BLUEPRINTS
Primary English
The Writing Book

Pie Corbett

Stanley Thornes (Publishers) Ltd

Do you receive BLUEPRINTS NEWS?

Blueprints is an expanding series of practical teacher's ideas books and photocopiable resources for use in primary schools. Books are available for separate infant and junior age ranges for every core and foundation subject, as well as for an ever widening range of other primary teaching needs. These include **Blueprints Primary English** books and **Blueprints Resource Banks**. **Blueprints** are carefully structured around the demands of the National Curriculum in England and Wales, but are used successfully by schools and teachers in Scotland, Northern Ireland and elsewhere.

Blueprints provide:
- *Total curriculum coverage*
- *Hundreds of practical ideas*
- *Books specifically for the age range you teach*
- *Flexible resources for the whole school or for individual teachers*
- *Excellent photocopiable sheets – ideal for assessment and children's work profiles*
- *Supreme value.*

Books may be bought by credit card over the telephone and information obtained on **(01242) 577944**. Alternatively, photocopy and return this **FREEPOST** form to receive **Blueprints News**, our regular update on all new and existing titles. You may also like to add the name of a friend who would be interested in being on the mailing list.

Please add my name to the **BLUEPRINTS NEWS** mailing list.

Mr/Mrs/Miss/Ms _____

Home address _____

_____ Postcode _____

School address _____

_____ Postcode _____

Please also send **BLUEPRINTS NEWS** to:

Mr/Mrs/Miss/Ms _____

Address _____

_____ Postcode _____

To: Marketing Services Dept., Stanley Thornes Ltd, FREEPOST (GR 782), Cheltenham, GL50 1BR

First published in 1994
First published in new binding in 1997 by:
Stanley Thornes (Publishers) Ltd
Ellenborough House
Wellington Street
CHELTENHAM GL50 1YW

98 99 00 01 02 / 10 9 8 7 6 5 4 3

A catalogue record for this book is available from the British Library.

ISBN 0–7487–3463–5

Typeset by Tech-Set, Gateshead, Tyne & Wear
Printed and bound in Great Britain by Redwood Books, Trowbridge, Wiltshire

CONTENTS

INTRODUCTION

The Writing Book is a structured and comprehensive bank of ideas, including 98 photocopiable copymasters designed to allow you to develop writing with primary-school children. It is concerned mainly with the compositional aspects of writing, rather than spelling, handwriting and punctuation. You will find a discussion of this approach at the start of the section on 'Teaching writing in the classroom' below.

This book covers all the types of writing that children need to undertake to meet the requirements of the National Curriculum in England, Wales and Northern Ireland, as well as the National Guidelines for English Language 5–14 for Scotland. You will find a detailed explanation of the coverage in 'National Curriculum links' on page xii.

The book has five main sections to provide complete coverage of all the key writing forms and skills. These are:

- 'Writing stories and poems' (imaginative writing in the Scottish curriculum)
- 'Writing for information' (functional writing in the Scottish curriculum)
- 'Writing from reading' (often called response writing)
- 'Writing from personal experience' (personal writing in the Scottish curriculum)
- 'Redrafting and proofreading'.

In addition you will find a clear discussion of strategies for teaching writing in the classroom, record keeping and assessment (the final redrafting section includes useful self-assessment sheets for use by the children, and a teacher's record-keeping sheet and accompanying prompt sheet to remind teachers of the key aspects of writing that need assessment), and a short bibliography of practical, straightforward books that will provide ideas for classroom activities. Since many teachers also like to link writing with topic work, a topic index has been provided.

Each of the five sections contains photocopiable copymasters, concise teacher's notes to accompany them and a bank of further ideas to get writing going. You will find that many real examples of children's writing have been included throughout. There are also occasional examples of the range and diversity of writing that can be generated with these classroom-tested ideas in the teacher's notes: these can be read to the class or used as further models or starting points to stimulate children's writing.

The copymasters are intended to be used across the whole primary age range and develop progressively within each section, beginning with ideas suitable for middle and top infants and becoming more and more difficult as the section goes on. Precise Key Stages have not been assigned to activities as their difficulty varies considerably from child to child and from class to class. Teachers will wish to use their own judgement as to what is appropriate for each child.

All the copymasters in this book are drawn from wide experience of successful classroom teaching, and the aim has been to provide a variety of approaches. You will find it useful to read the teacher's notes to get the most from each copymaster, but often you will have your own ideas about how to use the sheets. One of the advantages copymasters have over the traditional text book is that they can be written on: on many sheets pupils can underline, circle, edit, correct spellings and even cut up and reassemble. You will also find that many of the completed copymasters will make attractive classroom display material.

It is important to remember that developing writers should enjoy writing. The copymasters provide a set of activities that have already been proven in the classroom. Each copymaster will need to be introduced to the children with a clear explanation of the task required and the teacher will need to ensure that the work is carried out with care and commitment. Completed pieces of writing need to be shared and 'published' in displays or books. There is nothing like having a real audience to motivate writing!

TEACHING WRITING IN THE CLASSROOM

Understanding the writing process
My brother is financial director of a large company which makes bricks and tiles. Quite often when we go to visit him at home I've seen him using his small hand-held tape-recorder to dictate a letter. No doubt, on his return to work, his secretary types up the letter for my brother to sign. Now, who wrote the letter? My brother *composed* the letter whilst his secretary *transcribed* it:

he made it up and his secretary wrote it down. Of course, handwriting and spelling (transcription) support the communication of meaning (composition) but these are two different skills and you could be good at one and not at the other.

There is no doubt that for many children the business of sitting down to write is a complex and difficult job. There is so much to attend to and get right:

Where does the date go? Can I get the letters on the line? How do you spell this word? What shall I say next? How big should the margin be? Should there be a full stop? Indeed, the complexity of the act of writing makes one wonder that children ever get going!

Part of the difficulty is that children believe that when we (as adults) sit down to write we manage to orchestrate all these problems perfectly, straight away, to produce beautifully written, perfectly spelt, well-composed writing that needs no attention or readjustment of any sort. In reality this is not so at all. An important feature of breaking down this myth involves teachers rediscovering the excitement they felt when they first became writers by writing again and sharing the struggles, the difficulties, the first drafts, the abandoned attempts and the successes of their own work with the children.

To make writing an easier task we can encourage children to focus first of all on the *composition* – on finding the right words and the right structure. They should not worry about the *transcriptional* issues until the written work is to be made public. Looking at writing in this way certainly eases the tension created by a child wanting to 'get it right' and avoids concentrating on the secretarial skills at the expense of making up anything worth saying. **This book concentrates on developing compositional aspects of writing**.

It is interesting how, when you ask children questions such as 'What is the most important thing to think about when you are writing?', many will say things like 'the spelling', 'getting the date in', 'the margin', 'writing on the line', 'the finger gaps', 'doing it neat' and so on. Ask your class this question and see where their focus lies. This sort of answer reflects the messages we have given children about what matters when we write and about what makes a successful piece of writing.

Another reason for considering the compositional and secretarial aspects as separate issues stems from a careful reflection on how adults write. From the 1970s onwards the growing trend of inviting writers and poets into schools began to move many teachers to consider whether there was anything to be gained from children not just learning to write, but actually becoming writers. These teachers learned from working with writers various approaches to writing that might be adapted usefully to the classroom – brainstorming, revising, proofreading, publishing and ensuring an audience for writing were all ideas that reflect the ways in which adult writers work.

A consideration of how we write as adults underpins much of our present thinking about the possible ways children might develop as writers – this laced with careful note of what works for children and what does not. 'Good Primary Teachers pay attention to the process of writing, developed from a knowledge and understanding of the practice of experienced writers (including themselves); they are then able to provide classroom practices which allow children to behave like real writers' (*English for Ages 5 to 16* June 1989, para. 3.13). This belief was clearly a cornerstone of the original Programme of Study.

In both the Northern Ireland and Scottish documents a similar approach is required – emphasis is placed on the process of writing, the compositional and secretarial aspects and the importance of children writing for genuine audiences. The 'consultation report' that came from the NCC in September 1993 still hinges the approach to writing around the same notion. The strands in this document clearly identify the same concerns and beliefs.

This approach has lead to a view of the writing process that may be illustrated by the following diagram:

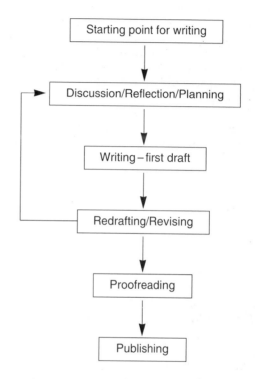

Each part of the process is discussed below.

Providing starting points

Children need to write for a variety of purposes and audiences, in a variety of different situations, so that they can have experience of matching style and content to audience and purpose. Some of these starting points will be determined by the teacher but there will also be opportunities for some to be determined by the children themselves. They will write letters, notes, diaries, newspapers, poems, stories and so on to friends and other children, for parents, the teacher, granny, even the school cook!

The copymasters provide a wide range of starting points and cover all kinds of writing. The first section looks at literary writing – stories and poems. The next section deals with the many forms of information writing. It touches upon diaries, letters, captions, labels, instructions, rules, recipes, opinions, adverts, greetings, lists, news, signs and reviews. The third section looks at writing in response to reading stories, poems and information, which is commonly referred to as response writing. Finally there is a section of ideas concerning personal writing based on children's own experiences.

Younger children will need to have the opportunity to play at writing and to imitate. They will need to see the teacher write in front of them on a regular basis. They will be motivated to write by the provision of writing opportunities in the home corner and writing area. Often just providing a postbox or some home-made booklets is sufficient stimulus.

The home corner

Older children need starting points that arise from their own reading and their own lives. The subjects chosen need to be manageable, interesting and challenging. They need to be rooted in something that the child knows and has something to say about. The subjects should also invite children to play with language and ideas.

Discussion, reflection and planning

Once a starting point has been thought of its function and form need to be considered and finalised: what is its purpose, who is it for, what needs to be said, what is the best format? Some initial planning and discussion of ideas and approaches may be useful. This could include considering how much time is needed and who will carry out which task. These early discussions may need to be recorded and noted.

As with any form of worksheet a copymaster will be unlikely to succeed on its own. It will need introducing and the children will need to use it within the framework of the writing process. Careful reading of the teacher's notes will assist you in this.

Moving straight into writing about an experience may prove to be difficult for many children (and adults). There is something to be said for leaving time for reflection and discussion before writing. This may provide an opportunity for writers to think around the subject, mull it over, sift ideas, discover their own viewpoint, see a way into the writing, listen to and use vocabulary, and discover what the experience meant for them. This early stage may act as a sort of linguistic bridge between the abstract experience and the concrete act of tussling with words on the page. To assist in this stage various tactics may help:

Discussion The traditional discussion about the subject lead by the teacher. In this the teacher often asks questions to get the children to 'rehearse' the sorts of things they might 'say' in their writing. This can also be done by putting the children into pairs or small groups to talk through or explain what they are thinking about saying and what they know about the subject, or to try out their story.

Image making Activities such as drawing, model making, painting, printing and so on can help children to focus upon a given starting point, internalise much of the detail, use appropriate language in passing talk and begin to discover what the image means to them. This might also apply to making music, dramatic activity, dance, mime and so on.

Brainstorming This can be carried out as a class, group, paired or individual activity. The aim is that those involved contribute as many ideas as possible over a short period of time. Anything is accepted. After seven or eight minutes the group then reflect on the various ideas, and begin to sift and organise them. This is a useful technique for quickly sharing thoughts and can unlock new ideas and stimulate creative thinking.

> Spiders
> Spinnerets translucent
> Abdomen tiny untidy
> Palps timid web
> crablike tarentula
> legs mouldy small
> blotchy evil velvety
> Slender
> Rapid telescope
> silky
> black fantastic
> reckless
> blue prickles spider
> dirty
> old knobbly
> Suculent leopard seaweed
> skinned

Brainstorming

Writing the first draft

Once there has been some consideration of the subject matter and appropriate planning then the initial composition begins. At this stage the child has to start to grapple with making up what to say as well as the problems of getting the words down on the page. A number of strategies can be used to help writers focus upon the composition and to make the transcription easier such as:

Scribing The teacher, another adult, a mature writer or another group member jots down what is being said.

Wordprocessor Pupils write directly on to the wordprocessor or an adult types for them. This is very useful for children who have difficulties in achieving a flowing handwriting style, because it enables them to produce a neat and legible copy. Research has shown that this has improved such children's self-confidence as writers and increased the amount they write.

Taping A small tape-recorder can provide the opportunity to come up with ideas and record them spontaneously, before any transcription is necessary.

Inventing spelling Encouraging children to invent their own spellings or to use a spelling line means that the compositional flow can be maintained. (A spelling or magic line is where a child may only be sure of how to spell the beginning of a word and uses a line to represent the letters they are unsure of. In this way a word like 'dog' might be written as 'd – –'. The correct spelling can be inserted later on.) The original National Curriculum documentation highlighted the importance of children being 'helped to be confident in attempting to spell words for themselves without undue dependence on the teacher.'

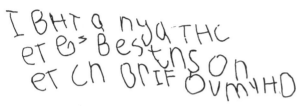

(I bought a new truck. It is [my] best one. It can drive over my hand.)

Invented spelling

Burst writing This technique involves putting pressure on the writer to write as much as possible in a very short period of time without paying attention to the conventions of spelling, punctuation and so on. This can release a sudden and surprising flow of ideas and is a useful way of overcoming writer's block.

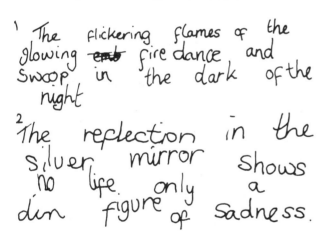

Burst writing

Redrafting and revising
If it is appropriate, the writing can be redrafted with a view to developing and reshaping the initial draft to make the communication more effective. Of course, you do not need to redraft a shopping list or notes, but a story or important letter may need such treatment. When redrafting the focus is still upon the compositional aspects, making sure that the piece of writing states what was intended in the best possible way. In order to redraft effectively it helps if the writer can see the piece of writing from a reader's viewpoint. Redrafting can be carried out:

With the teacher The teacher needs to sit alongside the pupils – individually, in groups or with the whole class – and talk through ideas for redrafting and reshaping writing, and changing, deleting and adding words, giving reasons for why certain changes make the piece of writing more effective.

In pairs Pupils can be paired together to redraft work, taking it in turns to act as editors for each other. **Copymaster 83** (Response partner) provides useful guidelines for this approach.

In groups When redrafting it is useful to get a reader's response. Story circles or topic groups can listen to each other's work in progress and offer advice on what seems to work well and what does not.

With teacher demonstration Writing in front of the class using a flip chart, OHP or blackboard provides a chance to discuss revisions to work.

With the whole class When reading children's work aloud the teacher can ask the children to identify the areas in the writing that are effective and that they enjoy, as well as the areas they think need development.

In the 'Redrafting and proofreading' section there are copymasters that give practice in revising stories and poems. When using these note that the writing and redrafting process can lead to various problems if not handled sensitively:

● There is the danger that children will change a few spellings and then write up their work neatly believing this to have been 'redrafting'
● There is no fixed number of drafts
● Not every piece needs to be redrafted
● Not all children redraft in the same way – the process has to be viewed flexibly.

First draft   *Final copy*

Proofreading

Once the work has been redrafted and the writer has decided that it is going to be 'published' – as part of a display, in a scrapbook, as a book in its own right or in a class anthology – then the proofreading process needs to begin. It is at this stage that pupils check for incorrect spellings and punctuation, and decide upon layout and presentation. It should be made clear that all these considerations are important because they help to communicate swiftly and clearly. The final product should be written in 'best' handwriting or typed, out of respect for the reader. There are copymasters in the final section 'Redrafting and proofreading' that concentrate on proofreading for spelling and punctuation, and consider the layout and organisation of writing.

Publishing

The final product should be shared with appropriate audiences that may well include friends and family. It should also be assured a place in the class library. At this point the purpose of writing should now become clear – to entertain, inform, persuade, and share thoughts and feelings.

Published books

Keeping the writing process flexible

Not every piece of writing needs to follow this pattern. Diary entries, personal reflections, notes, reminders, impressions, logs, writing used as a way of learning or thinking aloud and exploratory writing may not need to move through these stages. Some pieces of writing that we thought would lead to publication have to be discontinued – learning about writing also involves learning when to decide to abandon pieces that never get off the ground. It is also important to be quite clear that although I have outlined a writing process above, no two writers are comfortable using exactly the same strategies. Children need access to a variety of strategies and approaches, and they need to explore their own ways of becoming effective as writers.

If you watch children closely as they write and ask them what they are doing, you discover, for instance, that they all redraft in slightly different ways. Some children redraft in their minds *before* they put a word down, some redraft *as* they write. Some write a few words and

```
                    The Burning Bush.

The bush blazed, brightly before Moses.
A voice came to him.
Take off your shoes said he.
Who are you? Said Moses.
I am the God of this mountain said he.
Take off your shoes for this is Holy ground.
Moses came nearer no more.
He took off his shoes and knelt down before the bush.
The bush blazed like the white inside of the sun.
And yet Moses could see that the bush was unchanged.
Then God spoke one single word!
His name.
And power from God poured into Moses
As wine filling a cup.
*****
*****
```

'Best' work

then make changes, some write whole sections and then go back over them, and others write the whole passage before they go back to redraft. Personally, I like to use a variety of the above strategies at different times! Having fixed expectations would be akin to expecting every child to learn to talk or read in exactly the same way. This means that we need to introduce and demonstrate various ways of working, using the process described above as a guiding framework within which children can write.

As you can see this process will take time. What is envisaged by the National Curriculum is a situation where we ask our pupils to do less writing, but ensure that what we do is more meaningful, more purposeful and is brought to a conclusion that allows every child a full opportunity to say what they want to say and to capture their thinking on the page. At the heart of this approach is the recognition that much of the thinking and work can be done by the children, that many of the decisions can be made by the children, that often the children should decide what they will write about and how, and that children should be taught to reflect critically upon their writing, using appropriate vocabulary in order to improve its effectiveness.

The teacher will have to consider carefully a number of key decisions:

● How to find reasons for writing which are purposeful, meaningful and act as an invitation to engage with a written task. This may mean establishing a task that the teacher suggests or providing opportunities for the children to negotiate their own writing tasks
● What sorts of support and advice the variety of children will need in class
● How the writing will be published and who the audience will be
● What sort of process will be used and what needs to be organised to carry out the writing task successfully.

The copymasters will provide a backbone for developing writing ideas and redrafting and proofreading skills. Many of these ideas will need to be reinforced and built upon in the classroom using principles similar to the ones outlined above.

RECORD KEEPING AND ASSESSMENT

Each child will need some form of on-going profile to act as a record of achievement, showing the child's development across the primary years. The profile will be contributed to by the child, the parents and the different teachers. A complete profile should include:

● Factual details – such as medical records
● Teachers' observations – notes made in different situations
● Samples – a collection of examples that act as tangible evidence of development with teacher's notes attached
● Reflections – the child's own comments on progress made and future targets, as well as comments by parents.

The on-going use of the profile should enable the children to have an idea of their own development, ensure that parents are kept informed and can contribute to children's progress. It should also assist the teacher in planning appropriate teaching.

Such on-going records can become too bulky and time consuming to be of any use. Some schools have become bogged down with vast sheets covered in ticks that, at the end of the day, seem to tell us little about the child. It has to be remembered that the Level Descriptions/Statements of Attainment are only a very limited view of what we are hoping to develop in children. They are the more objective indicators, but development in writing has many other signposts en route which teachers will look for. In the Cox Report it was stated that 'the best writing is vigorous, committed, honest and interesting. We have not included these qualities in our statements of attainment because they cannot be mapped on to levels. Even so, all good classroom practice will be geared to encouraging and fostering these vital qualities' (June 1989). Considering the new Level Descriptions/Statements of Attainment, this comment becomes even more important to bear in mind.

Schools need to develop an approach that is useful, practical and informative. If evidence is gathered over a period of time this will provide a picture of what the child can do in a range of situations, and so enable teachers to confidently state at what level the child is working. It is important to remember that it is a child's *general* performance over a period of time that suggests a level of attainment, not one individual piece of work. A useful summary is contained in the Non Statutory Guidelines published in June 1990 in the chapter on 'Gathering evidence of achievement'. The annual guidelines for assessing writing at the different Key Stages give important guidance on the criteria to be used for deciding when a child has reached a level of attainment.

The writing conference

In order to build an on-going picture of the child's development and to use this information directly to move the child forward, teachers will need to hold regular writing conferences with children.

The writing conference is an opportunity to focus upon a child's writing development. The teacher may want to focus upon one particular piece of writing or perhaps discuss a folder of writing. Some possible approaches include the following:

● Let the child talk about their favourite piece
● Ask about the child's approach to writing i.e. how they set about the task
● Ask about the intended audience, purpose and form
● Get the child to take you through the various drafts telling you why changes were made. Try to get a window on to the child as a writer
● Find out if there is a point of growth you can identify together, a next development to work towards.

Comments and notes could focus upon the following:

1 Child's response
2 Content
3 Conventions – spelling/punctuation/handwriting
4 Process – planning, redrafting, proofreading and publishing
5 The next development.

Discuss any agreed point(s) and make this a focus for the child. Be careful about offering rules and definitions as a way of helping. Rules are abstract in nature and can only be understood in relation to a developing competence. *Show* the child how something is done – teach by illustration not definition. Look for patterns in errors and pinpoint any common, gross errors to work upon. Alternatively, ask the child what they would like to concentrate upon. Where useful, relate the child's writing to aspects of the reading the class has been doing.

Note down children's own responses to the selected piece or let them write a short note to go with it. Record the context – how the writing came about, who helped – and what this demonstrates about the child's growth as a writer.

Chosen pieces might be placed in the child's folder as being representative or interesting. They will need to have the note attached giving the context, teacher's and child's comments. The teacher's notes might indicate why the writing has been chosen and any aspects of the Statements of Attainment that this demonstrates.

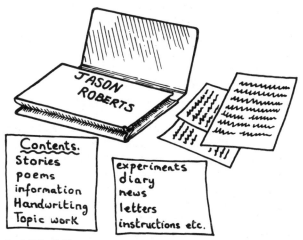

Contents.
Stories
poems
information
Handwriting
Topic work

experiments
diary
news
letters
instructions etc.

A child's folder

Date	Comments	Recommendations
21/1/94	J. read his story to me - fluently. Well structured - interesting ending. Re-drafted together.	J. to focus on finding engaging beginnings plus checking for full stops.
19/2/94	Looked at J's diary. Uses wide vocabulary. Full stops becoming a habit!	Proofread for spellings.

Teacher's notebook

A record of the discussion should be kept in order to build up a supportive picture of the child's development as a writer and any agreed recommendations. A checklist in a teacher's notebook might look like the example above.

Copymaster 86 (My writing) or **Copymaster 96** (Self-assessment) can be used by the children to assess their development over the course of a term or year. **Copymaster 97** (Writing record) can be used as a record sheet for writing conferences. **Copymaster 98** (Writing record prompt sheet) is designed to act as an aide memoire to teachers, highlighting key aspects of writing that should be noted.

Writing.

When I start to write a piece of writing I always build on a central idea, I prefer to work in quietness. If the piece of writing has to be good then I'm always concentrating. First of all I jot down ideas then I arrange them into the piece of writing. I then start to change words, I change non-interesting words for interesting ones. Make your work eye - catching and set it out so it looks good. Check for spelling mistakes. Never waste a good word, always try and fit it in. I like to read others work and grasp ideas from it. Look at ideas from all sides and find their best meaning and use. Use words that fit well in the piece of writing. Never stop concentrating, sometimes it helps to discuss your ideas with a friend.

Childs' comment on writing

NATIONAL CURRICULUM LINKS

Types of writing	Copymasters
Acrostic:	38
Adverts:	55
Aliteration:	22
Assessment:	97, 98
Audience:	56, 5
Bookmaking:	84
Book reviews:	54
Calligrams:	27, 28, 36
Captions:	44
Choosing words:	79
Contents:	62
Descriptions:	21, 23, 24, 30, 66
Diary:	13, 73, 76
Glossary:	62
Instructions:	52
Invitations:	45, 85
Labels:	16, 34, 72
Layout:	56–8
Letters:	46, 47, 59, 85
Lists:	41, 58, 65

Menus:	32
Messages:	14
Newspapers:	50, 51, 53, 61
Paragraphs:	56, 90, 95
Personal experience:	24, 68, 71–5
Planning:	3, 11, 19, 60
Proofreading:	83, 90, 95
Punctuation:	78, 83, 90, 95
Rapping:	40
Recipes:	42, 43
Redrafting:	77, 80, 81, 83, 88, 89, 92–4
Self-assessment:	86, 96
Sequencing:	1, 8, 10, 18, 35, 58, 59, 64
Signs:	48
Story endings:	7
Story grammar:	5, 20
Story openings:	2, 85
Story telling:	15, 63, 67
Traditional tales:	6, 9, 18, 81, 90
Word play:	25–8, 31, 33, 36, 37, 39, 69, 70

BOOKLIST

Catapults and Kingfishers, Pie Corbett and Brian Moses, Oxford University Press (1986).

A teaching handbook of ideas for poetry writing. Also a description of running a poetry writing session.

My Grandmother's Motorbike, Pie Corbett and Brian Moses, Oxford University Press (1990).

A teaching 'storehouse' of ideas for story writing covering the whole primary range plus a description of how to organise and run story writing sessions.

Does It Have to Rhyme?, Sandy Brownjohn, Hodder & Stoughton (1980).

Poetry writing ideas.

In Tune with Yourself, Jennifer Dunn, Morag Styles and Nick Warburton, Cambridge University Press (1987).

Poetry writing ideas and discussion of the teaching approach. Practical advice.

BP Teachers' Poetry Resources File for Primary Schools, The Poetry Society, 22 Betterton Street, London WC2H 9BU (1992).

Practical ideas in a loose-leaf file written by poets that visit schools. Updated with new articles each year.

Word Games and *More Word Games*, Sandy Brownjohn, Hodder & Stoughton (1985).

Lively approaches to developing word interest through writing and reading activities.

The Essential Guide to Poetry, David Orme, Folens (1992).

A lively collection of well-tested poetry ideas.

Did I Hear You Write?, Michael Rosen, André Deutsch (1989).

An interesting account of this popular poet's work in schools with plenty of ideas for poetry and personal writing.

TOPIC INDEX

WRITING STORIES AND POEMS

This section is designed to help children develop their ability to write stories and poetry. Children are invited to write individually, in pairs or in small groups, and in this way be influenced by each other as writers. There are activities to assist children in considering the sequence of a plot; that highlight story beginnings and endings; that emphasise planning and the consideration of setting, characters and situation before beginning to write; and that explore the importance of developing character, adding detail and using the solution of a dilemma as a storyline. Many of the copymasters act as imaginative writing stimuli.

The poetry activities highlight the importance of carefully selecting ideas and words. There are copymasters that encourage close attention to using the five senses, and to balance this there are activities that rely upon playing with words and ideas in a fun way. Writing poems as shapes is introduced as well as using rhyme.

STORIES

Copymaster 1 (Shopping tale)
Working in pairs, the children should look carefully at the sequence of pictures on **Copymaster 1**. They should then decide which order the pictures should go in. They could cut them out and re-order them, or number them on the page. The pictures could be stapled together and made into a small booklet.

Copymaster 2 (Starters)
The children read and choose which 'starter' they would like to use. Before they begin writing encourage the children to work in pairs. They should tell their partner what the story will be about, who is in it, where it is taking place and what will happen. Alternatively, they could draw their story as a sequence of pictures.

Copymaster 3 (Story questions)
The children should discuss with a partner and then fill in their answers to the questions. In this way it is expected that some planning will have occurred before children write their story.

Copymaster 4 (Supposing stories)
Many stories are based around the notion of 'What would happen if…' or 'Supposing…'. Use the opening lines on the copymaster to generate writing or to create more funny situations around which the children might write stories.

Copymaster 5 (Story builders)
Get the children to choose a main character, a place and an event to start their story going. They could cut out their choice and stick them into their story as illustrations.

Copymaster 6 (Fairy tale headlines)
The children have to complete the stories in the newspaper by cutting out the headlines and illustrations, sticking them on to a separate piece of paper and writing their accounts underneath.

Copymaster 7 (Endings)
The children could write the story that goes with the ending of their choice, working individually to begin with and then sharing their stories in pairs or small groups once written. They might then make up endings of their own and swop them. The children will probably need to have some time to talk about their story first, with the teacher or a partner, or to draw the action in cartoon form before writing as an aid to composition. Very small children could draw the sequence of the story and the teacher could then write it down.

Copymaster 8 (The magic box)
The story on this copymaster is being told through drawings. The children can tell each other how they would finish the story and fill in the empty boxes with their own pictures to show the end of the tale.

Copymaster 9 (Trolls)
This copymaster leaves space for the story shown to be added to and also leaves space for pictures. The story could be continued on further sheets, with the children weaving their writing and illustration together.

Copymaster 10 (Octopus story)
On each tentacle of the octopus there is a sentence from the start of a story. The children cut out the tentacles and put the sentences into the right order. This story may then be continued on further sheets.

Copymaster 11 (Story flow chart)
This copymaster is just a series of blank boxes linked together as for a flow chart. The flow chart can be used as an aid to planning. The children can either draw in the boxes or write briefly what happens next. Such a planner is also useful to ensure that key facts are not forgotten or that a sequence or process is in the right order.

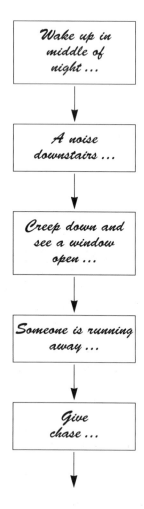

Copymaster 12 (Expedition 1)
Put the children into pairs or small groups. They are going on a treasure-hunting expedition but can only carry 10 kilograms between them. They should decide which ten items they will take.

Copymaster 13 (Expedition 2)
The map on the copymaster was found in the attic by one of a group of explorers and is very old. It shows an island where hidden treasure is buried. The story of the explorers' adventure is written as a diary, the first page of which is on the copymaster. Get the children to read the map and diary entry carefully and then continue the story in the same style.

Copymaster 14 (Messages)
The children should complete the empty and half-torn messages. Working in pairs or groups, they could share each other's ideas, pretending that they have found one of these messages. They could then write a story that includes this message.

Copymaster 15 (Bare bones)
This copymaster contains the bare bones of the beginnings of three stories. Put the children into pairs. First they have to help each other tell the stories, adding in detail and fleshing out the bare bones so that the brief reports of what happens become stories. The children could then move on to writing down the versions they have practised.

Copymaster 16 (Potion stories)
Get the children to complete the rest of the bottles' labels with magic potions. They should then write a story of what happens when they – or their friends – accidently swallow one of the potions. (Please give the usual warning and reminder to children not to drink from odd bottles, etc.)

Copymaster 17 (Magic wishes)
This copymaster can be used by children working individually or in pairs to record a secret wish – to change something, become something, acquire a super power and so on. All the wish boxes on the copymaster are filled in by each child/pair. Each wish is cut out and placed in a hat, out of which every child chooses one. The children write the story of what happens when they rub a magic cola can and a genie pops out to grant the wish they have chosen.

Copymaster 18 (Dustbin story)
A writer has accidently torn up and thrown into a dustbin the first part of a story. Working individually the children should cut out the different fragments and piece together the story. Then, in pairs, versions should be compared. Working on their own children should then continue the story. They should write into the rest of the story a pig that sings, a bad fright and three bags of gold.

Copymaster 19 (Story skeleton)
Written on to the skeleton are a number of key words from a story and there are spaces where extra words can be added in. The children complete the skeleton with special words that they would like to use and then have to write down their story. Stories should be read aloud to consider the differences.

Copymaster 20 (Story stealer)
Tell the children that the story stealer has a huge trunk into which all the stories that you know have been placed. The stories have become completely muddled up. The children should use the chart to jot down titles of stories they know, settings, main characters, events and endings. Remind the children in discussion of traditional tales as well as stories shared in school. They should then circle one part of each column to make up a mixed bag of ingredients which should be used to write a new story.

POEMS

Copymaster 21 (Rainbow poem)
The children should use the rainbow shape to write a sentence for each colour. They should begin by colouring in the key that shows the order of the colours. They then have to think of one thing to describe for each colour and write the sentence or phrase into the rainbow space. For instance:

'Chunks of butter on my bread' (yellow)
'Oranges are rough to feel' (orange)
'A cut finger' (red).

Copymaster 22 (Counting poem)
The children should read the poem carefully. What do they notice about the sounds? They should now use the opposite half of the page to try writing their own counting poem, making the words sound the same if they can. This is an early introduction to alliteration.

Copymaster 23 (Listen)
This copymaster could be used on a school outing or for writing outside the classroom – in the playground, on the street and so on. The children use the sheet to jot down the different sounds they can hear. Back in the classroom this sheet is then used as the basis for a 'Listen' poem. You may wish to begin the writing session by reading the children this example, written after a visit to a busy street:

Listen,
can you here the bus grumbling by?
Listen,
can you hear the milk float rattle?
Listen,
can you hear the jet roar overhead?
Listen,
can you hear the police car's siren wailing?
Listen,
can you hear the shoppers' feet clacking?
Listen,
can you hear the cars' engines grinding?
Listen,
can you hear the distant train toot?
Listen,
can you hear yourself think?

Copymaster 24 (I am afraid)
The first few boxes on the copymaster have drawings of frightening things happening. The children fill in the empty boxes with their own pictures of frightening things, adding labels if they can write. Working from these drawings, the children could write a list poem as in the following example:

I am afraid of scary spiders.
I am afraid of people who shout at me.
I am afraid of lions that could eat you.
I am afraid of when it is dark.

Copymaster 25 (Magic stocking)
The idea of the magic stocking is that you could have any present you would like in it and whatever it is can be made out of anything! Use the lists on the copymaster to begin getting ideas for a 'Magic' poem. Children should circle an item from the present list then draw a line to what it could be made of. Try to encourage the children to remember that it is a 'Magic' poem and that the more unusual the combination the better. For instance a doll made of plastic is boring but a doll made of sunbeams may be rather special! Once the children have chosen they can then write up their poem, borrowing the same format as this example and adding their own ideas.

In my magic stocking
I would like –
a doll made of white clouds,
a book made of flames,
a shell-suit made of banana skins,
a troll made of roof tiles,
a pair of ballet shoes made of butterfly wings,
a chocolate bar made of sausages,
a secret made of washing-up water,
a playground game made of liver,
a tie made of electricity…

Copymaster 26 (Crazy wishes)
This poem is similar to the 'Magic' poem above in that the idea is to dream up the most ridiculous and impossible wishes. I have begun by listing a few such wishes on the copymaster and the children should read mine and then continue the list.

Copymaster 27 (Sea word-picture)
This copymaster shows a seaside picture. The children have to write carefully on to spaces on the copymaster words that describe the different things shown. So, they may write 'jagged' in the space on the rocks or 'soft' in the space on the sand.

Copymaster 28 (Bonfire calligram)
A calligram is a picture that is made up of words. In this calligram the children are given the faint outline of a bonfire and some fireworks. The children should write appropriate words or sentences over the outline to actually create the picture, so that they are 'drawing' with the words.

Copymaster 29 (Animal poem)
I have written out half of this poem about animals but have left the children to try to find rhyming words to complete each verse. Children could then go on to think of their own animals and rhymes to accompany them.

Copymaster 30 (In our school)
This copymaster should be used to collect words and ideas for a poem describing lots of different things going on in the school. The children go round the school and record on the copymaster a list of things they'd like to put in their poem, made up of sounds they can hear, things they can see and things that people are doing.

The children should then work on each idea to make a list poem. You may want to read them this example:

In our school we heard –
children chattering while they worked,
pots and pans clattering in the canteen,
the school clock tick tock.

In our school we saw –
a photo of a blue whale deep beneath the sea,
a painting of yellow flowers,
a velvet curtain.

In our school we saw –
crows pecking in the playground,
Mrs Bancroft listening to children read,
the little ones dancing to music.

Copymaster 31 (Standing on my head)

This copymaster shows an upside-down poem! The children can use the phrase 'I am standing on my head' and repeat this, adding in reasons why they may be standing on their head. They could invent different linking phrases, such as 'I am hanging upside down'. Let the children do their rough draft on a separate sheet, using the copymaster to write down the final version. The following example could be used as an illustration of what is needed.

I am standing on my head
so that I can see the world from an ant's point of view.

I am standing on my head
so I can hold up the world.

I am standing on my head
because my new trainers are hurting.

I am standing on my head
in case I swallow my tongue.

I am standing on my head
so that I don't tread on any beetles.

I am standing on my head
so my trousers don't fall down.

I am standing on my head
because I was tired of standing on my own two feet.

Copymaster 32 (Menu poem)

This poem uses the format of a menu. Before writing on the copymaster the children should make notes and produce a first draft of a menu poem. This should be redrafted and proofread before it is copied out neatly on to the menu sheet. The children will need to decide for what occasion their menu will be used – a monster's party, a menu for making the teacher happy, a menu for making Dad mad? Below is an example which you could show children to give them an idea of what is wanted here.

Menu for making my teacher angry

First course
A delicious pâté made of squabbling children served on slices of warmly toasted spelling mistakes.

Main course
A well-roasted class fight in a sauce of rude jokes sprinkled with giggles.
This is served with mashed bad handwriting, boiled moans and groans and grilled pinchings.

Pudding
Straight from the freezer, an ice cream of fighting topped with a swirl of punches.

Copymaster 33 (The secret box)

Let children stick enlarged copies of the copymaster on to card and cut out the box template. On to each inside cover children should write a special secret. You may want to read aloud this list to stimulate the children:

Five secrets

1 My dad is Superman.
2 I keep a star inside my pillow.
3 A lamppost spoke to me this morning.
4 My cat can take his skin off.
5 I ate a slice of sunlight.

Before making the box the children should draw careful designs on the outside that have something to do with the contents. Children can then glue the flaps and fold the template together to make the box. When it is complete the secrets will be trapped on the inside – it will be a 'secret box'.

The children could write a poem about their secret box, saying where they found it, what it is made of and what it might contain. Ralph (nine years old) wrote the following:

I found my box
trapped in the centre of a star.
Its sides are made of
bees' wings and pollen.
Its lid is carved from
the rough tongue of a dragon.
Its hinges are made of
the jaw bones of a crocodile
I saw bathing in the sun's furnace.
If you press your ear
to the sides of the box
you would hear the buzz
of many insects.
My box contains
the secret of the wind's invisibility.

Copymaster 34 (Dragon's eggs)

Enlarge this copymaster before distribution. The dragon shown here has laid eggs. Each egg contains a baby dragon that has different feelings – get the children to think of a list of possible feelings (sad, lonely, hungry, angry, jealous, etc.). Under each egg the children write one of these feelings; inside the egg they write down how their dragon will behave. So, an egg that is labelled 'angry' could have 'crushes villages in a spurt of fury' written inside it . An egg labelled 'sad' could contain 'curls up and cries tears of gold'.

Copymaster 35 (Jumbled poem)

The lines and words of this poem have become quite jumbled up in my computer. The children should cut up the lines and try to reconstruct the poem, adding any extra words that are needed.

The following is my version. The children will create many different variations; as long as the poems make sense they are valid, though some, of course, may read more effectively than others.

Owl

Owl
was darker
than ebony –
flew through the night,
eyes like amber searchlights,
rested on a post,
feathers wind-ruffled,
stood stump still,
talons ready to seize
and squeeze.

Owl
was death
for it flew through the dark
that swamped the fields,
that tightened its knot,
that bandaged the hills
in a blindfold of fear.

Owl flew – Who – Who – Who –

Copymaster 36 (Spider calligram)
Using the faint outline of the spider the children write their chosen sentences on the spider's legs so that the words make the drawing. I have done one leg. Before writing on the copymaster they should make a list of useful words, phrases and ideas. These may be written as sentences or just as words.

Copymaster 37 ('Odd Kettle of Fish')
This poem consists of everyday phrases that have had their meanings taken literally. Once children have read the poem, they should spend several days collecting sayings and phrases of their own. These should then be displayed on the wall and the children can try writing their own poems. *Brewer's Dictionary of Phrase and Fable* (Cassell) is a useful source of sayings. Here are some to start your list:

laugh your head off/like a hyena
slam the door in your face
silence is golden
look a gift horse in the mouth
it's raining cats and dogs
as quiet as mice
over the moon.

Copymaster 38 (Animal riddle acrostic)
The riddle on the top half of the page is an acrostic, with the key word, 'Badger', hidden in the centre of the poem

in bolder print. On the lower part of the copymaster the children should begin their own acrostic by writing the subject of their poem – an animal – down the centre. Each line is then built on either side of one of the letters that spell out this animal.

Copymaster 39 (Open door)
The children should colour each door in a different colour in faint pencil crayon. The children should make a list of things that are the same colour as the doors. There should be a yellow one, blue one, green one, red one and so on. Then they write the first draft of a poem for each coloured door on a separate piece of paper, redraft this and proofread it, before copying it neatly on to the doors on the copymaster. So, for a blue door, children may write:

Beyond the blue door
are skies that stretch,
seas that roll by,
a flash of the kingfisher,
stripes on a parrot fish,
school jumpers
and a sad moment.

Joanna (eight years old) wrote on her red door:

My red door
is blood from a cut,
Tanya's hair,
a streaky sunset,
our school jumpers,
when Dad is angry,
building bricks
and post office vans.

Copymaster 40 (School rap)
Use this copymaster as a worksheet to carry on with the school rap I have begun. The children could work alone or in pairs. They should insert the school's name into the space provided and continue the rap on the copymaster. As they write, they should try to maintain the same rhythm. The teacher may need to try out several with the whole class. To help with the rhythm the children will need to say the rap aloud to 'hear' if it sounds right. Raps can be presented as performance pieces with percussive background. Children will need time to prepare and practise their raps. To write other raps use a simple format such as:

Hip hop hap
it's the football rap

or

Hop hip hap
it's the disco kid rap.

FURTHER IDEAS

Stories
Use postcards of paintings or posters to start a story. Seaside and holiday images tend not to work well –

however, people, scenes, events and places can be used successfully. Lay the postcards out and let the children choose one which appeals to them. This can then become the front cover for a story they are about to write or be an illustration in the story itself. I have found that some of the Surrealists' pictures, in particular, intrigue children.

Use music to start a story or poetry writing. Select a piece that you feel may be atmospheric or exciting and get the children to listen. They can start writing as they listen or afterwards.

Dress up a child in a costume and get the other children to decide who the child might be, what they are like, where they come from and what has happened. This information may then be woven into a story. Alternatively, the teacher could determine some of the information about the character and start telling the children a story with the character in it.

Bringing in objects. Use an object to start a story. For instance, bring a mirror into class and tell the children that it is a magic mirror which, if you gaze into it, can enable you to see into the future. You could also use keys, boxes, rings, a ship in a bottle and other intriguing items. Suggest a few ideas to get the children going, for example 'What does this key unlock?', 'What secret is held inside this box?', 'If you put this ring on what might happen?'

Writing 'on location'. Most writing takes place inside the classroom. For a change, take the children out – to a church, a park, an old cinema, the playground – and use this as a starting place for a story. What happens, who comes along? I have had successful writing from visiting churches, a turkey farm, an old house and a hay field.

Retelling a tale but changing one aspect. A useful way into this idea might be to read one of the many children's stories based on traditional tales such as *Clever Polly and the Stupid Wolf* by Catherine Storr. In such stories a traditional tale has been taken and parts of it altered – a princess becomes a boy, or a wolf becomes gentle. The children will need to take a tale they know well and alter a character, the setting, some of the events or the ending.

Inventing a huge lie. In a way all stories are huge lies, so making up lies itself can lead into stories. For instance, you could tell the children that you came to school on an elephant this morning and it is parked at the back of the school. Ask the children to invent a similar 'whopper' and, having invented the lie, consider what might follow as a consequence.

Stories about what happens when children swop places for the day with their mum, dad, brother, sister, best friend or teacher.

Tape-recording stories. Instead of children writing let them use a tape-recorder to tell their stories; the finished version should be played back to the class. Some children will wish to retell the stories having heard their first version.

Telling a story in a circle. Put the children into a circle.

The first person begins a story – 'Once upon a time there was a girl called Jane' for example – and each child takes it in turn to add the next sentence. This activity can be great fun.

Drawing a story before or instead of writing. This can be done as a cartoon or as a single illustration. It is suitable for very small children who cannot write or for much older children who struggle with composition.

Stories based on books read. For example having read *Mrs Pepperpot* children imagine they are small.

Stories about discovering a magic ring or key. What power does it have? What might happen?

Let the class know several days in advance that you want them to write a story and ask them to 'find' one. The children may want to ask parents, neighbours, friends or grandparents. The story could be true or a traditional tale.

Leaving a secret message on the class newsboard – for example you may leave a message which says 'HELP! I AM TRAPPED, signed Laura'. This message should be used by the children as the start to a story. The children should consider where they found the message, who it is from and what happens.

Putting a storyteller's hat in the bookcorner. Whenever you read or tell a story put on the hat. Leave it for the children to try.

Stories about giants or fierce monsters that need defeating.

Telling a story with a contrast – sad clown, happy ogre, frightened lion, giggly dragon and so on.

Making a sign: 'DO NOT ENTER', 'DO NOT TOUCH'. Where is it, why is it there, what happens if you ignore it?

Stories about being trapped or in a cave.

Stories about being lost.

Useful first lines

● The door creaked open and Sally sat up in bed.
● The egg had definitely begun to crack open.
● John picked up the stone. It glowed in his palm.
● The trees in the forest sighed. The King had died and his only daughter was to be Queen.
● In the land of Gooder there is a place where you can see into the future. If you dare. When Kim stared into the future pool she saw...
● He hadn't meant to steal but...

Poems
Collecting playground rhymes.

Secrets – 'It's a secret but
      my Dad is Superman.'

Dreams – 'I dreamed I was ...'

Would you rather – 'Would you rather be a funny person
        have a new bike or …'

Magic Box – 'In my magic box
      I would have
      a burning sun
      the moon melting …'

Flying – 'If I had wings I could feel …
     If I had wings I could see …
     If I had wings I could touch …
     If I had wings I could be …'

What you are – finding different ways of comparing parts of the body.

  'Your head is like a round football.
  Your eyes are blue as the sky.
  Your nose is like a white pear …'

Weather – the rain, snow, storms, wind and hot sun are all potent stimuli for writing.

People – describing unusual people.

Places – describing special and secret places. Looking at the landscape, taking notes on the roadside. Listing things that are happening:

  'A man drives home in his Peugeot,
  dice dangling in the rear window.
  A new grandmother waits at the bus stop,
  a baby's shawl in her bag …'

Without you – listing things that might happen if someone left:

  'Without you peanuts would loose their crunch,
      my brain would turn to mud,
      ants would rule the world …'

Don't worry – 'Don't worry if the world floods with rain,
      if windows start to cry,
      if Superman turns into Donald Duck …'

I want – listing impossible and real wants:

  'I want to touch
  a blaze of lightning.
  I want to write a dream
  that never ends.
  I want to destroy
  the evil in people's hearts …'

You make me feel – this idea is a chance to use rhyme. It comes from a poem by Adrian Henri, as does the 'Don't worry' idea listed above.

  'You make me feel like a coyote's thumb
  You make me feel like Big Daddy's tum.
  You make me feel like a pound of cheese.
  You make me feel like a plate of peas.'

Counting rhyme – 'One, two, three, four
        Monsters knocking at my door …'

Riddles – getting the children to focus on a subject and jot down a list of its attributes: the things they know and notice about it. The secret of a riddle, remind them, is to give a list of clues without giving away what the subject is.

Sounds – describing noises. Imagine it is night-time. The children hear a noise. What could it be?

  'Who is there?
  Is it the midnight fox
  searching the dustbins?'

Alphabet poems – A ate an apple, B bit a banana, C caught a carrot and so on. The poems could be about food or an event, for instance a visit to the sea:

  'A arrived on the beach.
  B built a sandcastle.
  C caught a crab.
  D dug a pit.
  E …'

Seasons poem. Under a heading for each season the children write a list of all the seasonal events they can think of. For example:

  'In winter –
  The snow smothers the trees,
  icicles hang like frozen fingers,
  bright lights sparkle in shop windows,
  tinsel decorates the Christmas tree,
  carols are sung on the telly …'

Night poem. Brainstorm a list of words and ideas to describe the sights, sounds and events of night-time. Read Abdul's poem as an example:

At night
the shadows slither
down dark streets.
The lights in the flats
shine like a ship.
People queue at the chip shop.
Cars sneak by.
Their bonnets shine
like polished shoes.
Behind the curtains
TV mumbles on.

Teaching tips
●   Before the children write, read out one or two examples – preferably by other children.
●   When writing a poem that uses a repeating phrase, such as 'without you …', always do one or two lines with the whole class so they understand what you want.
●   End sessions by hearing some of the children's work read aloud.
●   With younger children use a flip chart and transcribe for the group. You should do this often.

Shopping tale

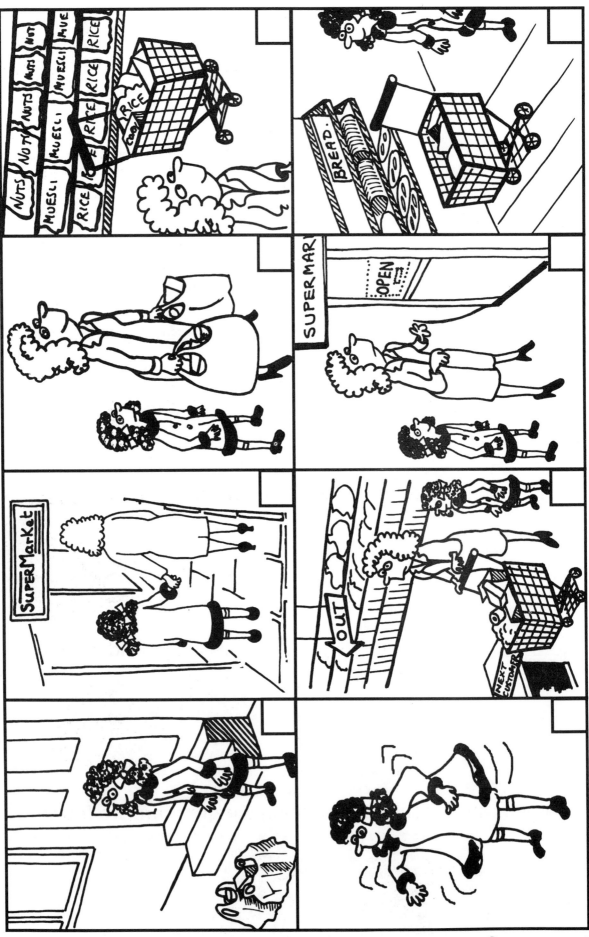

Starters

'Come back,' shouted the old man.

Once upon a time there was a beautiful woman who lived all alone in the middle of a forest.

I woke up and could hear something scratching at the door.

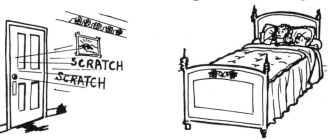

On our way to school this morning we found a golden ring.

There was a giant who lived near our village and he had a terrible temper.

We were late for school but when we got there we found that ...

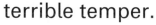

Copymaster 2

9

Story questions

What title could you give your story? Try out several possible titles.

What are the names of the main people in your story?

Where does the story take place?

What time of day is it?

What is the weather like?

How does the story begin? Try out your first line here.

Copymaster 3

Supposing stories

Supposing you woke up and found that you had become really small…

Supposing you turned into a cat or a dog…

Supposing you could make yourself invisible…

Supposing your best friend turned into a monster…

Copymaster 4

11

Story builders

Characters

Places

Events

Copymaster 5

12

Fairy tale headlines

 FAIRY TALE TIMES

Princess catches thieves

Wolf is defeated

Prince finds treasure

Trolls
found
in
woods

Copymaster 6

Endings

So, the children ran out of the cave into the sunshine. They still held the old man's bag. They sat down on the sand to see what might be inside.

The unicorn said goodbye and spread its wings to fly home.

Miss Fussy said that she would never teach Class 2 again.

Jo said she was sorry to Mum and this time she meant it.

Sam lay down on her bed.

It was great to be home.

'I'll never tell another lie.'

The fox sniffed the wind and knew that spring would soon arrive.

Copymaster 7

The magic box

Copymaster 8

Trolls

When the sun set it was dark in the forest. Soon the animals were fast asleep. Only the trolls were awake. They were busy building a boat.

All night long they fetched wood and banged nails. When the morning came they took their new boat down to the river. Now they would be able to cross it.

Octopus story

The sun was shining on his new car.

Billy had his breakfast and ran outside.

A seagull sat on his roof.

Billy was very cross.

He got into his car and set off for the seaside.

On the sands he played with all his friends.

Billy the Octopus looked out of his window.

He bought an ice cream and a bag of chips.

Copymaster 10

17

Story flow chart

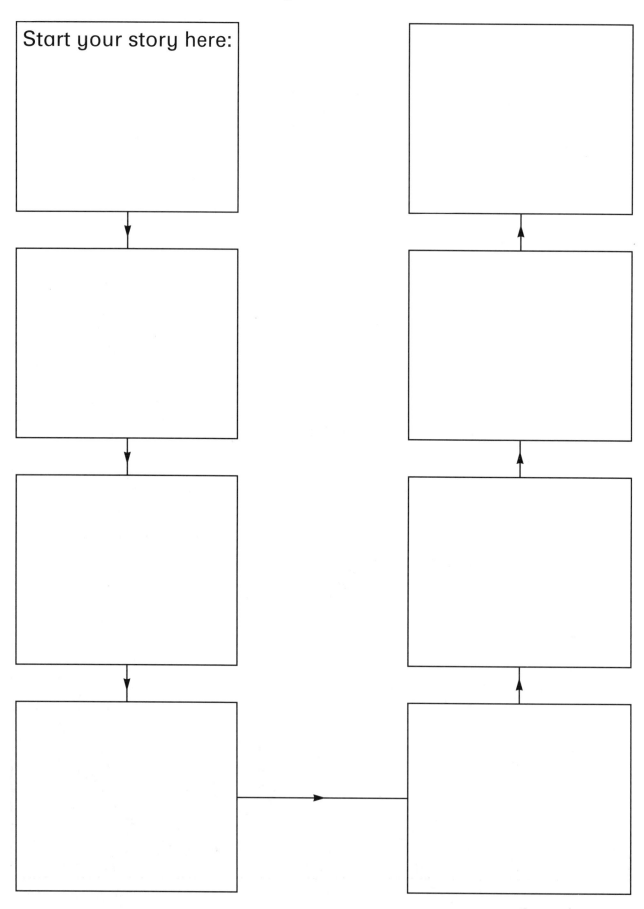

Start your story here:

Expedition 1

3 kg

2 kg

1 kg

1 kg

$\frac{1}{2}$ kg

$\frac{1}{2}$ kg

$\frac{1}{2}$ kg

$\frac{1}{2}$ kg

3 kg

4 kg

1 kg

$\frac{1}{2}$ kg

4 kg

2 kg

$\frac{1}{2}$ kg

Copymaster 12

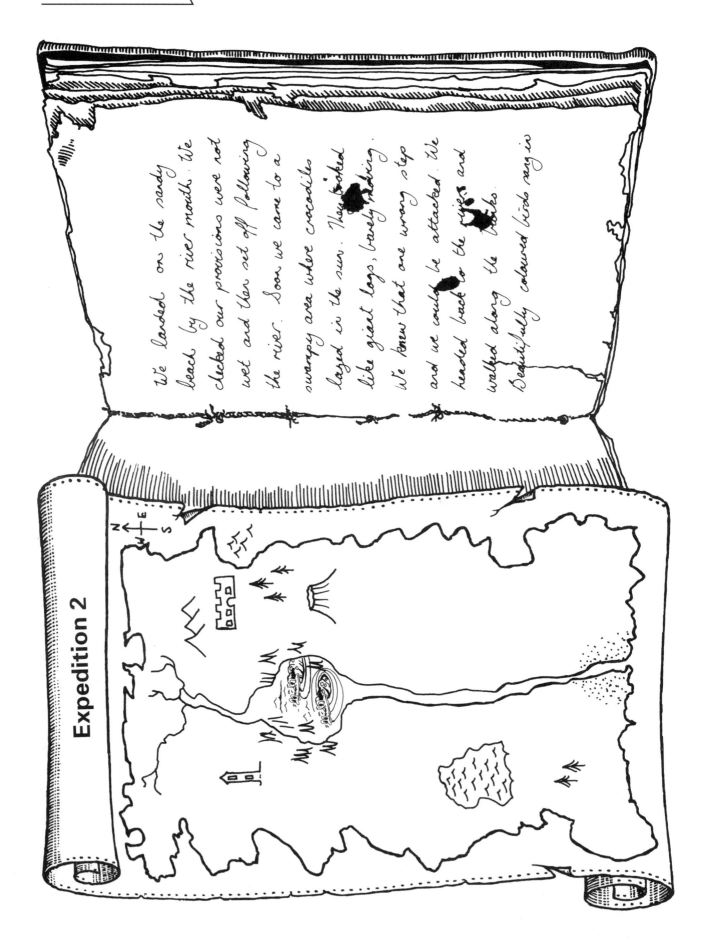

Expedition 2

We landed on the sandy beach by the river mouth. We checked our provisions were not wet and then set off following the river. Soon we came to a swampy area where crocodile layed in the sun. They looked like giant logs, barely moving. We knew that one wrong step and we could be attacked. We headed back to the ships and walked along the docks. Beautifully coloured birds rang in

Copymaster 13

20

Messages

If you know
good for
meet me
midn

Help! I am
stranded on
Boot Island.

Don't speak to the
man at the sweetshop.
I know where the
money is hidden.

found the
outside door
and you
night

LOST AT SEA.
NO FOOD OR
WATER.
LAST
SEEN NEAR

Copymaster 14

21

Bare bones

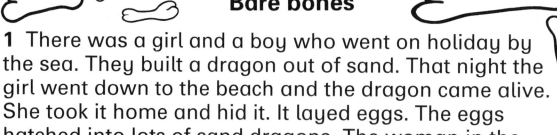

1 There was a girl and a boy who went on holiday by the sea. They built a dragon out of sand. That night the girl went down to the beach and the dragon came alive. She took it home and hid it. It layed eggs. The eggs hatched into lots of sand dragons. The woman in the house where they were staying was very tidy. She got cross with the children because there was sand everywhere. So the children tried hiding the sand dragons …

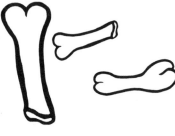

2 There was a girl who was always in trouble at school. One day she drew a pair of glasses on a poster of Henry the Eighth. Her class teacher caught her doing it. She made her stand outside the headteacher's door. While she was standing there she saw someone stealing money from the head's room and sneaking out of a window. She ran after them …

3 The Queen had a daughter who never smiled, so she said that whoever made her daughter smile could have as much treasure as they could carry away. So lots of people came to the castle to try to make the girl laugh. They told jokes, they told funny stories, they did silly dances, they played tricks. But she did not laugh. Until one day a poor boy came to the palace. He had a parrot with him …

Copymaster 15

Potion stories

Moonbeam Cream ◡ Turns children into their teachers for the day.

POWDERED STARDUST
1 gulp and you fly.

RUB SUNLIGHT LOTION ON TO BECOME INVISIBLE

INTERPLANETARY PILLS
One for mindreading powers.

Drink Jupiter Juice for X-RAY vision

Dab on toad ointment for extra strength

Magic wishes

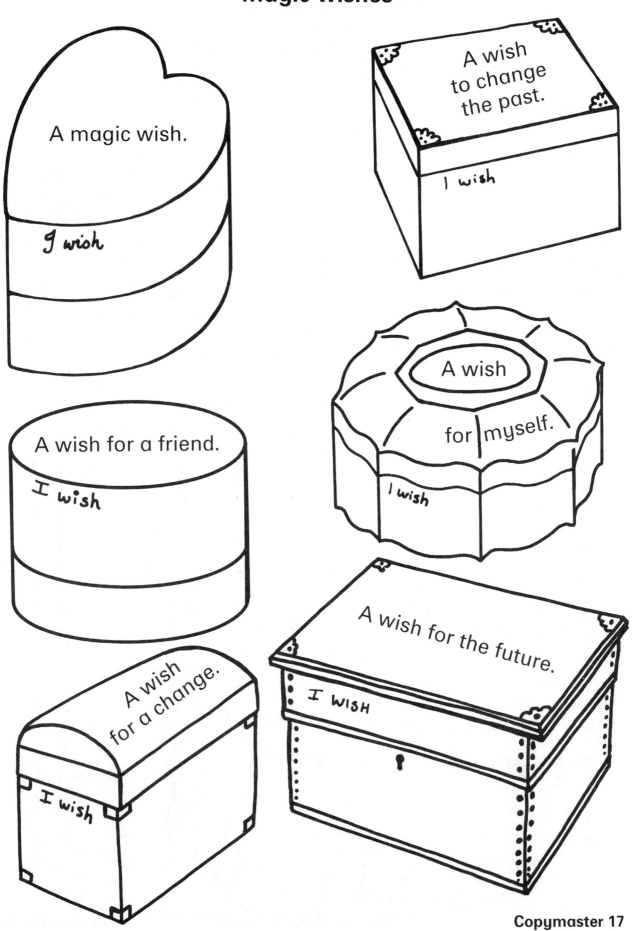

A magic wish.

I wish

A wish to change the past.

I wish

A wish for a friend.

I wish

A wish for myself.

I wish

A wish for a change.

I wish

A wish for the future.

I WISH

Copymaster 17

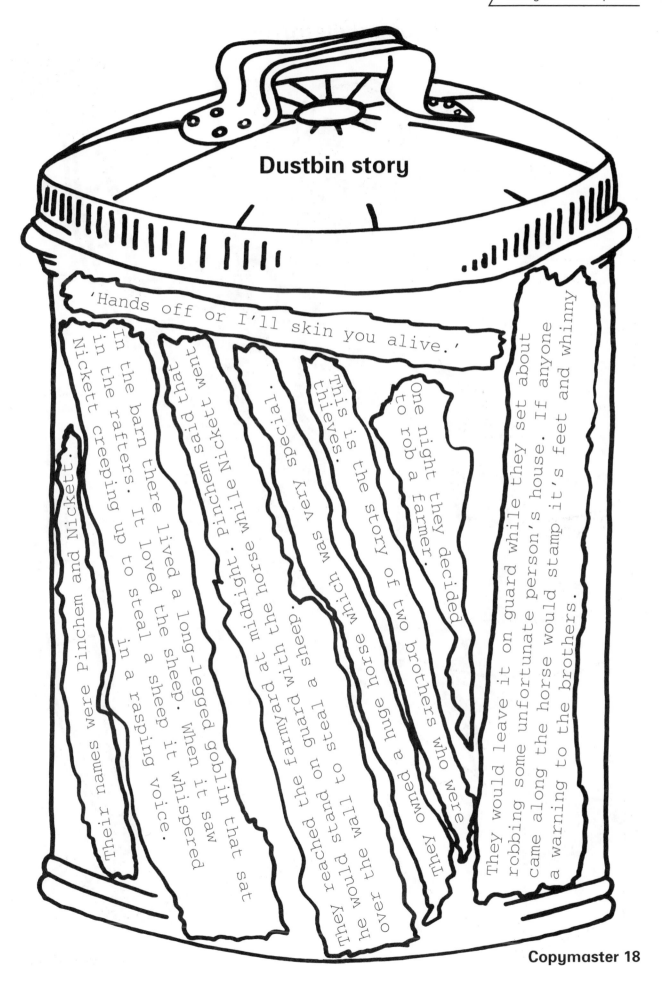

Dustbin story

'Hands off or I'll skin you alive.'

Their names were Pinchem and Nickett.

In the barn there lived a long-legged goblin that sat in the rafters. It loved the sheep. When it saw Nickett creeping up to steal a sheep it whispered in a rasping voice.

Pinchem. Nickett would want that special midnight horse at the farmyard with a very special sheep.

They reached the farmyard on guard to stand and steal a sheep. He would wall to over the huge horse which was owned a farmer.

This is the story of two brothers who were thieves.

One night they decided to rob a farmer.

They would leave it on guard while they set about robbing some unfortunate person's house. If anyone came along the horse would stamp it's feet and whinny a warning to the brothers.

Copymaster 18

25

Story skeleton

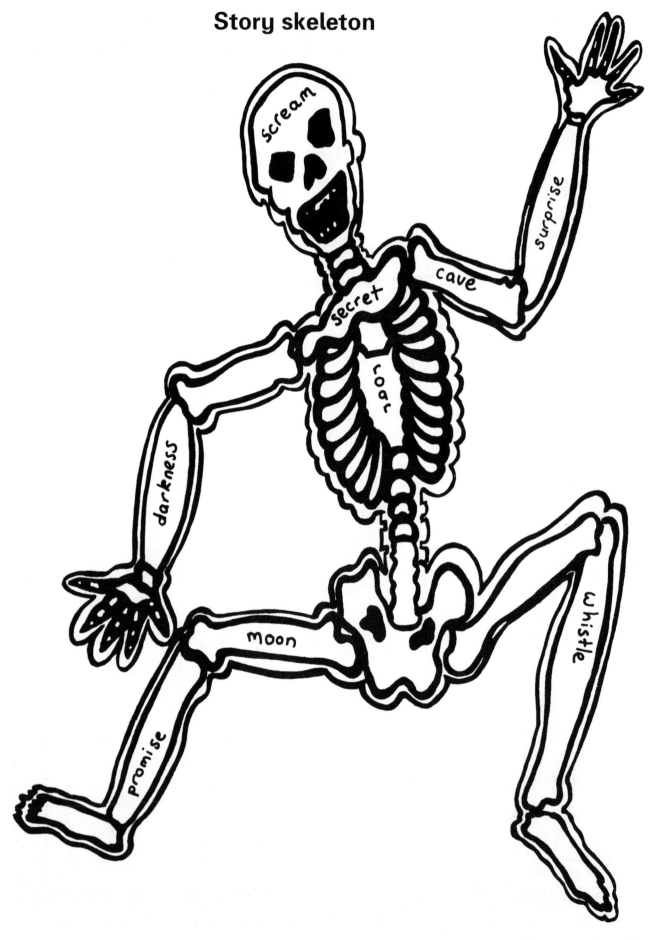

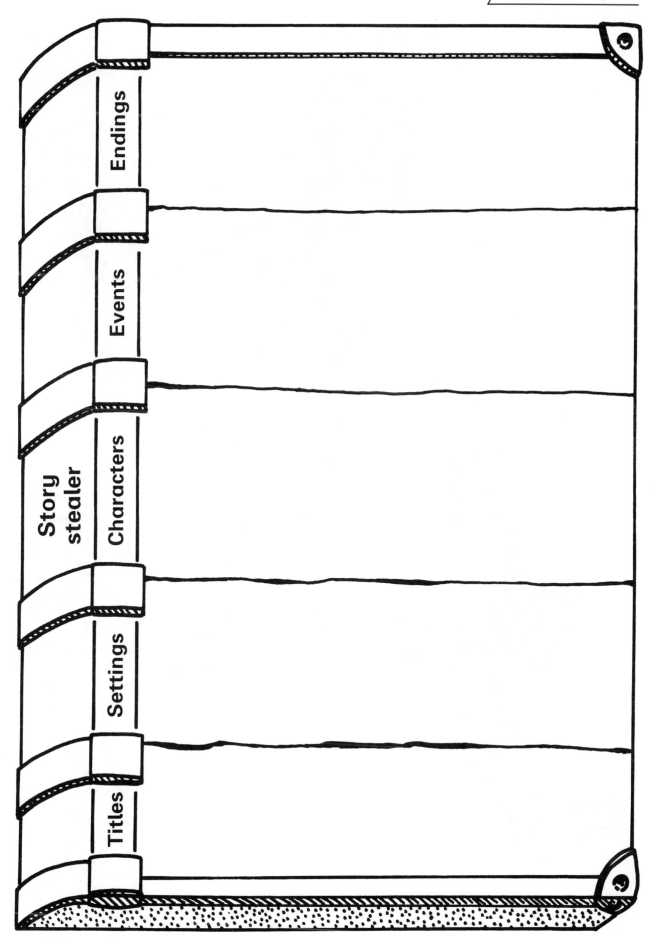

Story stealer

Titles

Settings

Characters

Events

Endings

Rainbow poem

Key

☐ red
☐ orange
☐ yellow
☐ green
☐ blue
☐ indigo
☐ violet

Counting poem

One   One white whale went for a sail.

Two   Two tiny trees sat on their knees.

Three   Three thirsty thieves collected leaves.

Four   Four fat frogs sat on logs.

Five   Five funny foxes sat in boxes.

Six   Six silly sweets started to tweet.

Seven   Seven silent sausages started to scream.

Eight   Eight late plates opened up the gate.

Nine   Nine naughty newts dressed up in suits.

Ten   Ten tired toads crossed the road.

Copymaster 22

29

Place I'm in:

Listen

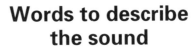

What is making the noise?

Words to describe the sound

Copymaster 23

I am afraid

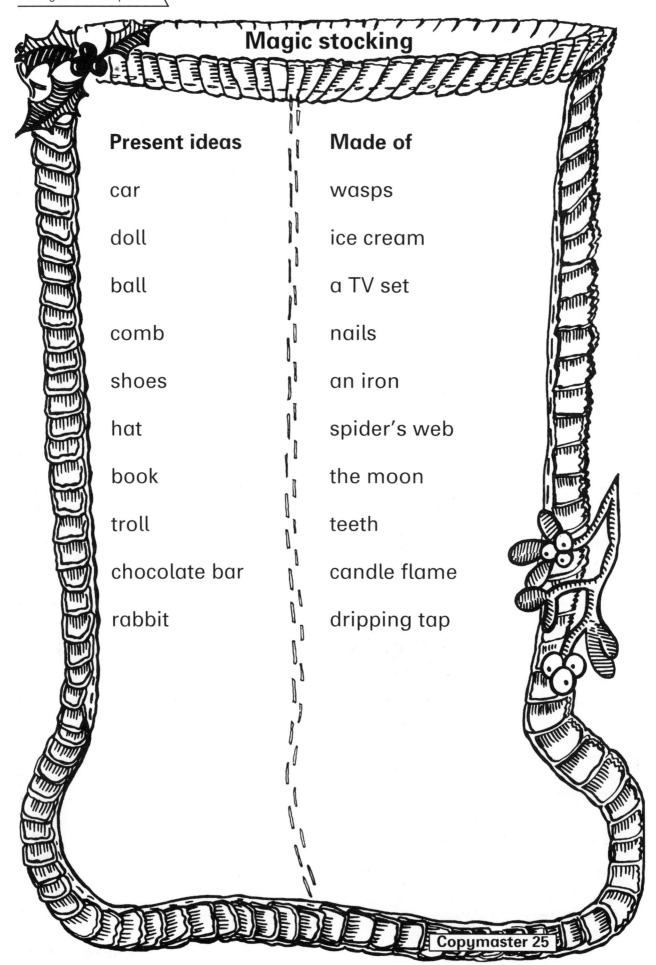

Magic stocking

Present ideas	Made of
car	wasps
doll	ice cream
ball	a TV set
comb	nails
shoes	an iron
hat	spider's web
book	the moon
troll	teeth
chocolate bar	candle flame
rabbit	dripping tap

Copymaster 25

Crazy wishes

I wish I was a mouse
scuttling for safety.

I wish I could fly
over the roof tops.

I wish …

Copymaster 26

33

Sea word-picture

Bonfire calligram

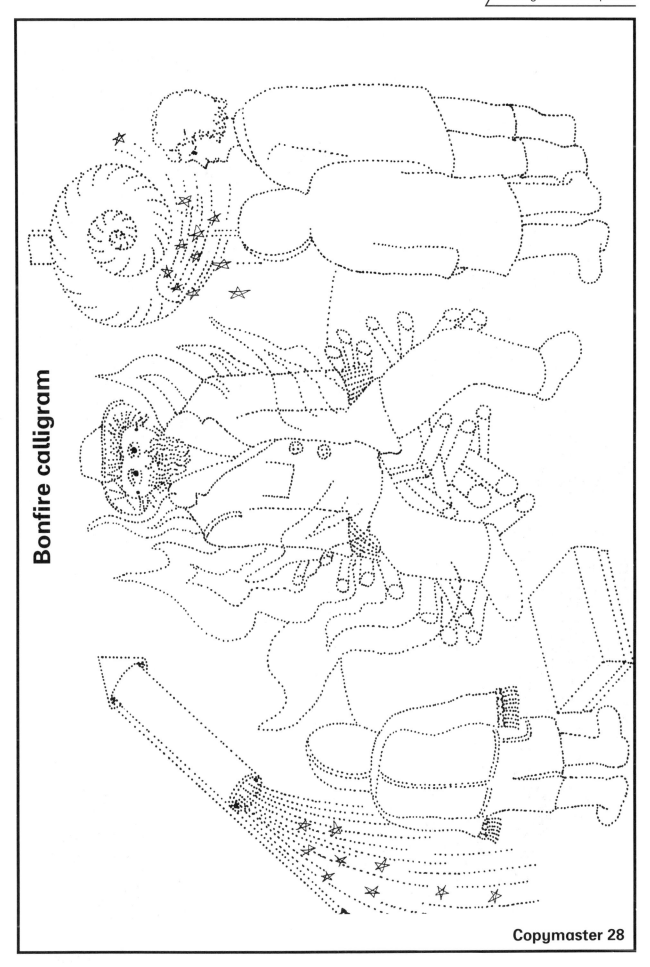

Copymaster 28

Animal poem

Imagine a snake
thin as a ...

_____

Imagine a cat

_____

Imagine a pig

_____

Imagine a dog

_____

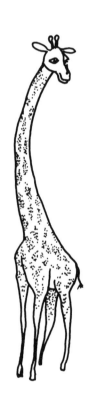

Imagine a flea

_____

Imagine a giraffe

_____

Imagine a bear

_____

Imagine a seal

_____

Copymaster 29

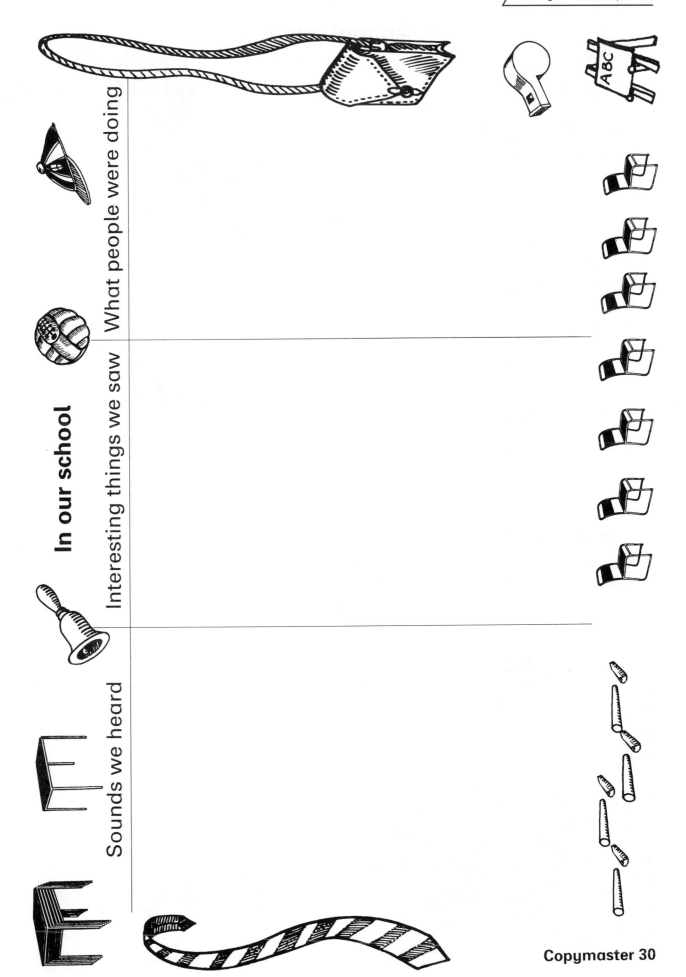

In our school

What people were doing

Interesting things we saw

Sounds we heard

Standing on my head

I am standing on
my head

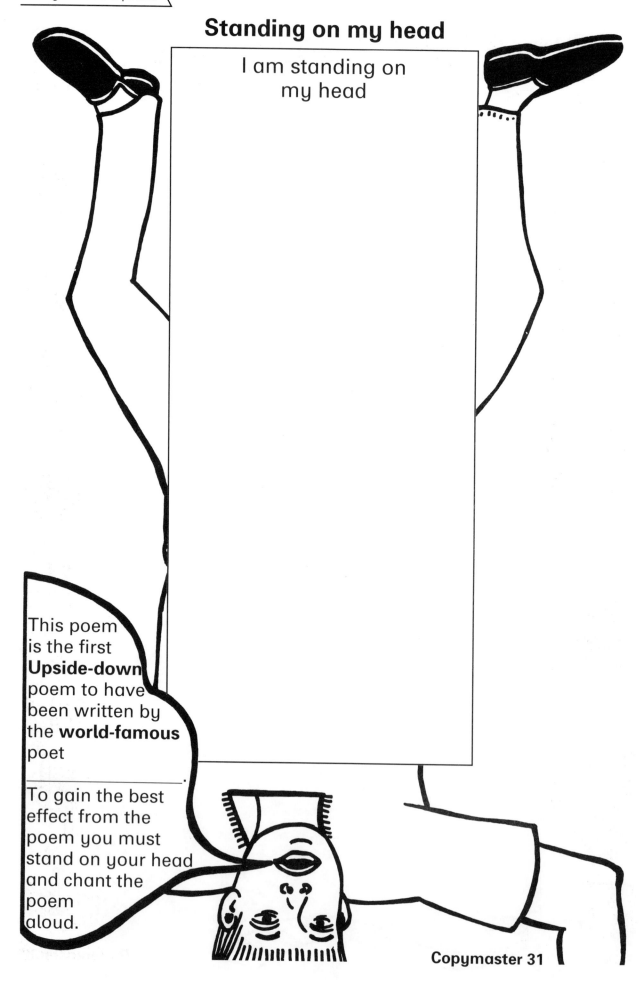

This poem is the first **Upside-down** poem to have been written by the **world-famous** poet

_____.

To gain the best effect from the poem you must stand on your head and chant the poem aloud.

Copymaster 31

  **Menu poem**

A menu for_____

 First course

 Main course

 Pudding

Copymaster 32

The secret box

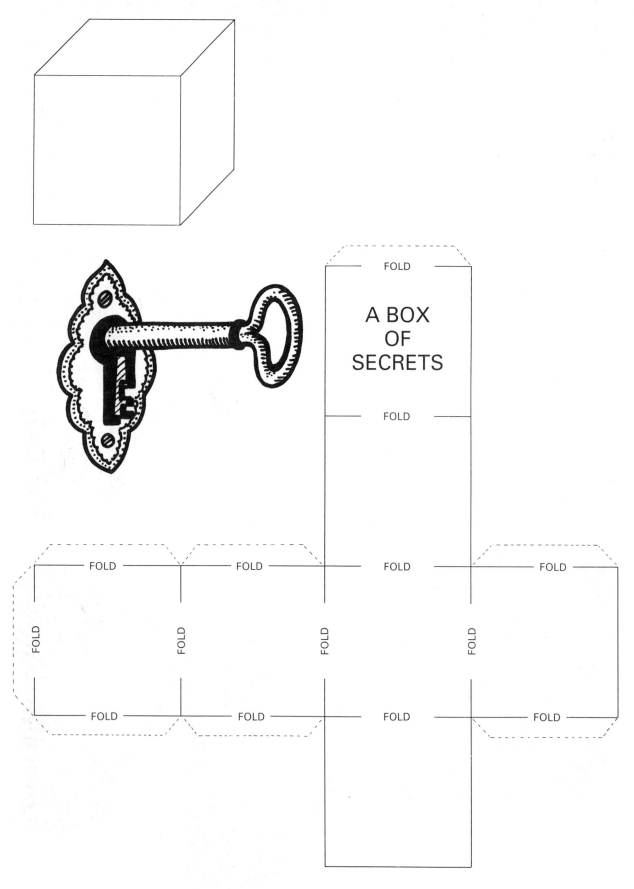

A BOX
OF
SECRETS

FOLD

FOLD

FOLD

FOLD

FOLD

FOLD

FOLD

FOLD

FOLD

FOLD

FOLD

FOLD

FOLD

Copymaster 33

Dragon's eggs

Jumbled poem

was death

was darker

that bandaged the hills

eyes like amber searchlights,

Owl

than ebony –

rested on a post,

in a blindfold of fear.

that swamped the fields,

flew through the night,

and squeeze.

OWL

that tightened its knot,

Owl

for it flew through the dark

feathers wind-ruffled,

Owl flew – Who – Who – Who –

talons ready to seize

stood stump still,

Copymaster 35

42

Spider calligram

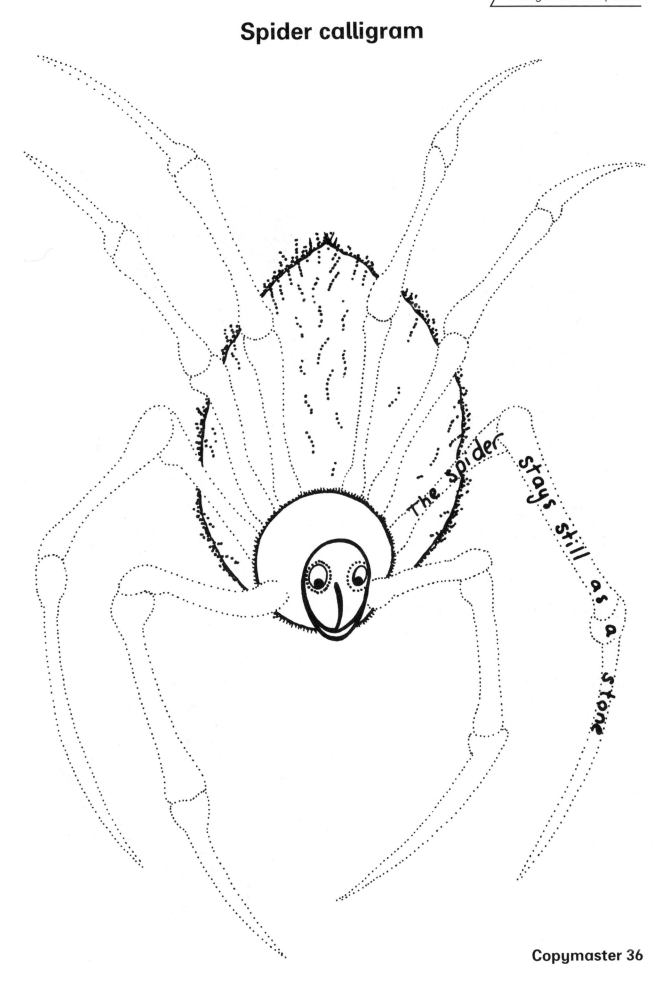

The spider stays still as a stone

'Odd Kettle of Fish'

1 The detectives said that
The books had been cooked.
(They tasted good.)

2 My teacher said we could
have a free hand.
(I added it to my collection.)

3 Some people bottle up
their feelings.
(I keep mine in a jar.)

4 My mother said –
'Hold your tongue!'
(It was too slippery.)

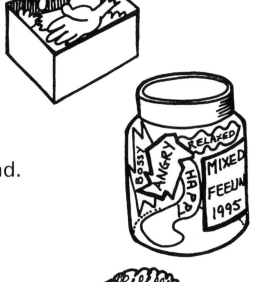

5 When my sister laughs
she drives me round the bend.
(I catch the bus back.)

6 Dad told me
to keep a stiff upper lip.
(It's in a box by my bed.)

7 My uncle is a terrible
name dropper.
(I help my aunt
to sweep them up.)

8 In the school races
I licked everyone in the class.
(It made my tongue sore.)

Copymaster 37

Animal riddle acrostic

Like a small **B**ear
       bundles over the dark road.
Brushes p**A**st the front gate,
       as if she owns the joint.
Rolls the **D**ustbin,
       like an expert barrel rider.
Tucks into yesterday's **G**arbage,
       crunches worms for titbits.
Wak**E**s us from deep sleep,
       blinks back at torchlight.
Our midnight feaste**R**,

       ghost-friend, moon-lit, zebra bear.

Copymaster 38

Open door

School rap

Hip hop hap
it's the ———————————— school rap

We like to do our very best,
we hardly like to take a rest.

Hip hop hap
it's the ———————————— school rap

Our teachers call us funny names,
we like it best when we play games.

Hip hop hap
it's the ———————————— school rap

Copymaster 40

WRITING FOR INFORMATION

This section introduces writing in a range of different forms – recipes, captions, greetings cards, letters, news items, signs, lists, instructions, adverts and information. Consideration is given to ensuring that children think about the audience and purpose and how these affect the form, content and layout. Some copymasters require children to think about sequencing and to change text to make it easier for a certain audience to read. The particular demands of different forms of information writing are highlighted through children using the copymasters in this section, sharing what they have written and critically considering each other's approaches. Children are introduced to the notion of using headings and to terms such as 'glossary' and 'contents'.

Copymaster 41 (My life list)
Down one side of the copymaster is a list of facts about the life of a girl called Daisy. The children have to select some facts from their own lives and complete the second column. This could be extended by children adding on other pieces of information about themselves, through either writing or drawing. Older children could design their own 'passports'.

Copymaster 42 (Muddled recipe)
The children need to look carefully at the pictures and then read the recipe statements below each picture. These have been muddled up. The children could cut out and reassemble the recipe, sticking the finished piece on to a clean sheet. This activity could lead on to writing or drawing recipes when doing classroom cooking. It introduces the idea of the term 'recipe' and leads into the activity on Copymaster 43.

Copymaster 43 (Funny recipe)
This recipe copymaster is an invitation to make a recipe for creating a new person. The children should read the recipe poem in pairs. They then decide what sort of person they would like to make and should list the ingredients, look in a recipe book and list the sorts of words and phrases used in recipes, for example 'take a pinch of, add a slice of, stir, let this simmer, place in a hot oven' and so on. The recipe should be written in the space provided on the copymaster. This could then be cut out and mounted. A class book of recipes could then be made.

Copymaster 44 (Captions)
This copymaster requires the children to look carefully at the pictures. For each picture they have to write a caption to describe what is happening.

Copymaster 45 (Invitations)
The children have to read the top half of the copymaster which is an invitation to a monster's party. They can then decide on the sort of party they themselves would like to hold. The bottom half of the copymaster is for the children to complete their own party invitation.

Copymaster 46 (Fairy tale postbag)
Read aloud with the children the two letters from the fairy tale characters. The children should then write a reply to each one.

Copymaster 47 (*Golden Goose Chronicle*)
Get the children to reply to this letter which appeared in the fairy tale newspaper. There is space on the copymaster for a reply, or a separate piece of paper could be used.

Copymaster 48 (Street signs)
This copymaster shows a street scene with various blank signs and notices. The children need to discuss what the signs might be for and choose their words carefully to fill them in.

Copymaster 49 (Animal lists)
This is a simple activity where the children have to draw a line from the animal to the adjective which best describes it. The children can only make one choice, so they will have to consider which word they think is best. Beside each animal they should then write a sentence on the line provided using the words, for instance 'The cool cat purred'.

Copymaster 50 (Picture news)
On this copymaster the children have to write or tell the news item that goes with each picture.

Copymaster 51 (Draw it)
This is the reverse of the above activity. Here the children have to draw the illustration that goes with the news. They need to read carefully in order to draw what has been written about. Drawings could be compared and discussed.

Copymaster 52 (Instructions)
The picture shows two children arguing over a game. Nearby is a skipping rope, a ball and a hopscotch game. The children decide on their favourite playground game and in the space provided write the rules for playing it. The completed copymasters should be swopped around so others can read the rules and see if they are clear enough for them to play the game.

Copymaster 53 (Spot the bias)
This copymaster invites the children to read the newspaper article and spot the bias in the writing, namely that the journalist obviously favours one football team over another. In pairs the children should read the article carefully and underline any word or phrase that they think is biased. This should be followed by a rewrite of the news report in the space on the copymaster or on a separate piece of paper in one of two ways: a) biased in favour of the other team; b) in as fair a way as possible.

Copymaster 54 (Book recommendation)
This copymaster can be used for children to complete after reading a book they have enjoyed. It is intended that they should record information on this sheet that would be useful to others looking for a good read. The copymaster should go into a folder kept by the library entitled 'Recommended reads'.

Copymaster 55 (Adverts)
On this 'noticeboard' there are a number of blank 'for sale' signs so that the children can advertise friends, teachers, characters from books and so on. One is filled in as an example.

Copymaster 56 (Layout)
This copymaster contains some basic information about China that needs to be set out better. The children can draw lines on the sheet to indicate where they would break the text into paragraphs, and add a title for each section in the margin. Alternatively, the children can cut up the text into sections, pasting them on to a fresh sheet underneath the titles they have thought up. This information should then be rewritten with pictures for a different audience – younger children, another class, as a letter for a friend or as a holiday brochure.

Copymaster 57 (Rewrite)
The piece of information on this copymaster has been written for older children. The task here is to produce a simplified information sheet for a class of seven- or eight-year-olds. The children should underline pieces that will need changing. They need to think of titles for different sections and decide which parts will need illustrating. Finished versions should then be compared and given to younger children to see if they can enjoy the new text!

Copymaster 58 (Information list)
Sally has been looking in reference books and has made a list of facts that she has found out. At the moment the information is muddled up – the children should work on the list, organising the facts into groups. The information can then be written up as interestingly as possible as a fact sheet.

Copymaster 59 (Computer error 1)
The computer has made a terrible mistake with printing out this letter. The children have to cut the letter up and reassemble it so that it makes sense.

Following is one of the possible versions the children might end up with – though other variations may make good sense as well.

```
Wildlife Safari Park,
Kimpton,
Sussex.

Dear Joanna,
I am writing to thank you for your recent
letter. I am pleased that you enjoyed your
visit to the Wildlife Safari Park.

You are right to point out that we do run
a conservation programme. We aim to
rehabilitate animals. It is our aim to use
the park to ensure that endangered species
can survive. We also hope to educate the
public. If it is fun as well then that is
an extra bonus.

Once again I am pleased that you arrived
home safely from your visit and thank you
for your kind words.

Yours sincerely,
Jane Carter.
```

Copymaster 60 (Headings)
This activity is about making a fact sheet for your own school. The child on the copymaster has begun by thinking of some headings to write about. The children have to sort the headings shown into a sensible order. Some headings should be dropped if they aren't appropriate. The children should then use their study skills to discover more about each heading and write a fact sheet for the school.

Copymaster 61 (50-word items)
The challenge of this copymaster is that the editor of the newspaper shown has only got two 50-word spaces left. The children should write on the copymaster in the spaces provided in 50 words or less. The class could then be divided into editorial groups. The 50-word stories should be read aloud and voted on for interest and clarity. Groups should vote to see which are the best-written stories and justify their choices.

To extend the activity, children could invent their own headlines and swop them over with a partner, before writing another 50-word news report.

Copymaster 62 (Glossary and contents)
Down the left-hand side of the copymaster is a list of words from a glossary. The children should complete the space provided by writing down what the words mean. Reference books (e.g. *The Aztecs* by R. Nicholson and C. Watts, Two-Can, 1991) may be needed here! The right-hand side lists the contents. In the space provided the children should write down what subjects they would expect each item to cover. This could be followed by the children being given a book title such as 'The Greeks' (or a title relevant to a topic the children have just covered). They should then produce a glossary and a contents list for a reference book on this subject. This will give you some insight into what was learned from the topic!

FURTHER IDEAS ▶

A newsboard–children can write at home and pin things up in class.

A class scrapbook for children's home writing or to publish 'best' pieces.

Drawing or painting 'news' items.

A class diary–a different child to write in it every day.

Writing letters to other classes inviting them to watch a class show or presentation related to work that is underway, or a short play or a reading of poems or stories.

Writing letters to the headteacher thanking him or her for visiting the class show.

Writing letters organising a school/class outing and thanking those who helped or who have been visited afterwards.

Writing thank you letters to parents and helpers who listen to children reading.

Writing letters to local newspapers/radio stations. These might be about special events or activities in school or relate to local events or concerns. For instance, a Cardiff primary school wrote to the local waterboard complaining about pollution in a nearby river. They were invited to watch the council pull a car out of the river!

Writing letters to authors whose work has been enjoyed – these might contain questions as well as comments on the author's writing.

Using *The Jolly Postman* by Janet and John Ahlberg to generate fun letters based around traditional tales. For example, Lucy wrote a letter to the big, bad wolf:

Dear Mr Wolf,

I am concerned that you have been seen hanging around the park recently. My sister and I often play on the swings and we do not wish to be eaten up. If you carry on with your bad ways we will have to send for the local wolf-catcher and you will be put in a home for bad wolves.

Yours sincerely,

Lucy, nine years old.

Designing a boardgame and writing instructions for it.

Writing instructions for classroom needs–e.g. keeping the bookcorner tidy, feeding the class gerbil etc.

Writing lists of what children know before doing a topic.

Writing lists of what children have learned after a topic.

Writing captions to go with displays and pictures. Captions could be in the form of statements or questions.

Putting labels on displays, belongings and equipment. Children become used to labelling items indicating who they belong to or what they are for.

Writing invitations for class and school events.

Writing greetings cards for key festivals and special occasions.

Making posters concerned with school rules–e.g. 'Please walk, don't run' etc.

Using writing to plan, jot down and order ideas. Demonstrate this in front of the children.

Persuasive writing–writing opinions and arguments. Show children how to organise the pros and cons.

Describing people–friends, relatives, old people, unusual people, special people.

Describing places–local places, holiday resorts, seaside places, towns, villages, woods, secret hiding places, markets, libraries, churches, cinemas, funfairs etc.

Describing events–at the doctor's, the school fête, the school concert, a wedding, sports day, going greyhound racing etc.

Using different types of books as models for children to learn from. Let them read part of Roald Dahl's auto-biography *Boy* and then write up some incidents from their own life.

Writing a 'Did you know' book related to a particular topic. Every child could contribute a number of pages, each one beginning with the words 'Did you know …?' The rest of the page is about an interesting fact to do with the project.

Writing an 'Is it true?' book. Each child can contribute two sides. On the first side the children write a fact followed by the words 'Is it true?' Over the page is the answer plus an illustration and perhaps one more interesting fact. For example, from an 'Is it true?' booklet on birds:

Humming birds got their name because they can hum tunes. Is it true?	No, but they can hover like a helicopter

Making a simple pamphlet about the topic in hand–this may mean writing an information booklet for a younger class about the area being studied. Children should consider how the needs of the younger audience will affect the writing and presentation.

Writing an information poster or fact sheet. In pairs the children select a topic and write a series of questions they would like to find the answers to. They use reference books to discover the answers and present this information on a poster or small fact sheet. These could be displayed on the wall or duplicated for each class member. For example, one class wrote a series of fact sheets on outer space–one sheet for each planet.

My life list

Daisy's life list

I was born in 1989.

My birthday is in April.

My hair is fair.

My eyes are blue.

I am 98 centimetres tall.

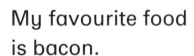

My favourite colour is blue.

My favourite food is bacon.

I live in a cottage.

I have a cat called Choco.

My hobby is kite flying.

My best friend is Melanie.

Your life list

Copymaster 41

51

Muddled recipe

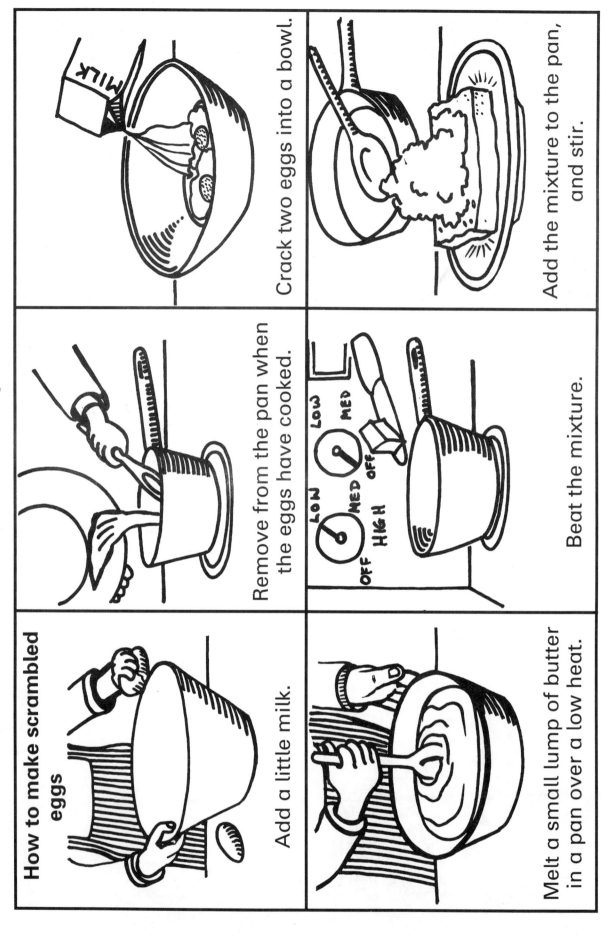

Crack two eggs into a bowl.

Add the mixture to the pan, and stir.

Remove from the pan when the eggs have cooked.

Beat the mixture.

How to make scrambled eggs

Add a little milk.

Melt a small lump of butter in a pan over a low heat.

Copymaster 42

52

Funny recipe

RECIPE

This person is made of baked tuna and brown rice.

Her hair is made of boiled spaghetti hoops
and slices of cucumber.

Now add in a hamburger for her face.

To make eyes stir in pickled onions.

Let this simmer with carrots for a nose.

Place in a hot oven.

RECIPE

This person is made of ...

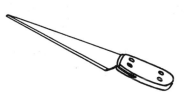

Copymaster 43

Captions

Invitations

Dear children

Please come to our Monster Party.
It is on Tuesday 22 June 1999.
The party starts at midnight.
It will be held at The Bat Cave on the Ghoul's Beach, Hastings Town.
Please come dressed as a dreadful creature.
The party finishes at dawn.
We hope you will enjoy our Dinosaur Donuts.

Love from Dotty.

Dear _____

Please come to _____
It is on _____
The party starts at _____
It will be held at _____
Please _____
The party finishes at _____
We hope _____

Love from _____

Copymaster 45

55

Fairy tale postbag

Dear Wolf,

We are all fed up with you chasing us around. You have blown 2 of our houses down. We are scared of going out in case you eat us up. Why can't you be friendly or take a long holiday in Australia?

Love,
the little pigs

Dear Hansel and Gretel,

I am sorry that you ran away from my lovely little house made of sweets. I cannot think why you did not want to stay.

I am baking a lovely pie to eat and wondered if you would like to come and see me soon.

Love from,
the kind old lady
xxx

Copymaster 46

Golden Goose Chronicle

Price 6 p.

Dear Sir,

I am writing to complain about the theft of two magic pots which I had hidden in my kitchen. One of my pots was called 'Plenty' and if you asked it to cook, it would boil you up a pot of porridge. My other pot was very special. If you put one thing in you would pull out two of the same! If anyone has seen these pots please let me know,
Yours sincerely,
Jack the Piper's cousin.

Reader's reply:

Copymaster 47

Street signs

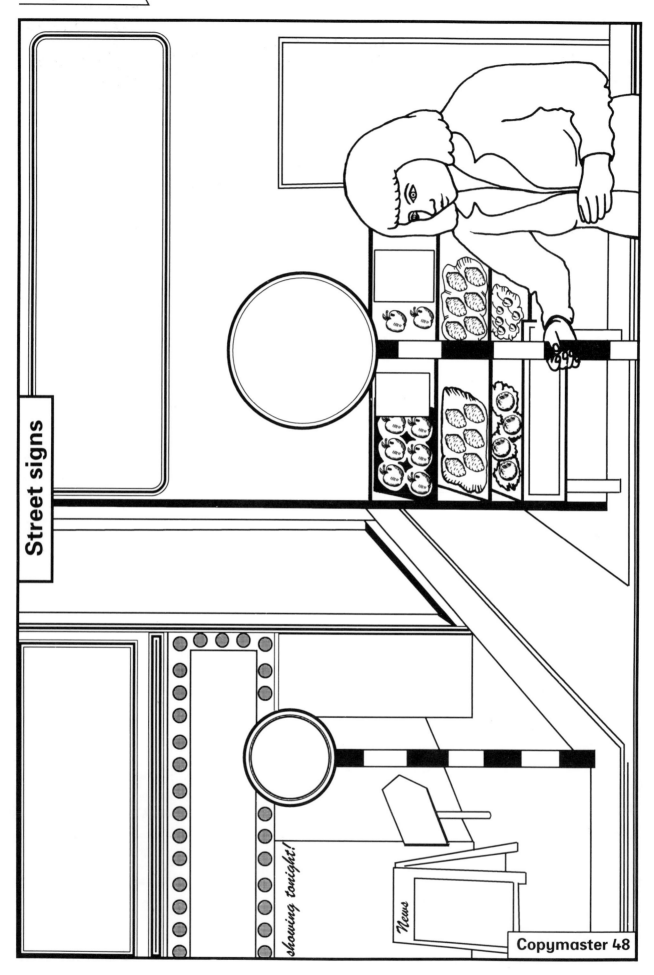

showing tonight!

News

Animal lists

Animal	Description	Write a sentence
cat	tiny	_____
dog	cool	_____
bear	furry	_____
zebra	cuddly	_____
snake	fierce	_____
tortoise	shaggy	_____
monkey	slithery	_____
tiger	slow	_____
porpoise	stripy	_____
ant	bouncy	_____

Copymaster 49

59

Picture news

LION AT LARGE!

SCHOOL CROC SHOCK!

Draw it

PRINCESS PRESENTS PRIZES

On Friday afternoon two children from Ethelbriggs Road School won a painting competition. The children had to paint a picture of their favourite animal. The Princess of Wales presented the prizes of £10 each to the winners. They were Lucy Luck and Ron Deering, both aged seven years old. The prizes were presented in the local gardens where the Princess also saw the roses and flowers in bloom. She enjoyed an ice cream and saw the ducks at the boating pond. Afterwards the children said it was great to meet a real princess.

Copymaster 51

Instructions

Rules for playing _____

Spot the bias

ROVERS – TEAM OF THE MATCH

Last night Rovers played against Wolves. From the beginning Rovers played superbly despite losing four unlucky goals. Their striker, Dunne, was unfortunate to be sent off when he made an excellent tackle. Throughout the game Rovers found themselves defending against Wolves and were beaten by some lucky strikes. Johnson, playing with the wind in the wrong direction, defended his goal at all times against the attackers. The Wolves' attackers got away with an off-side which the referee missed. Rovers tackled well despite several warnings and managed to shoot at goal no less than ten times. There were a number of lightning shots by the Rovers' attackers which only missed because of the wind direction.

Copymaster 53

Book recommendation

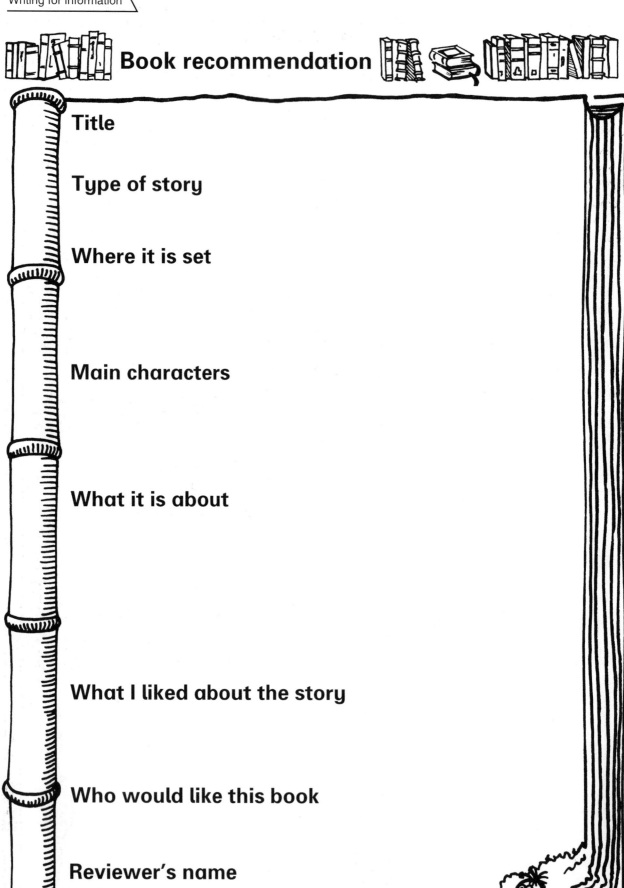

Title

Type of story

Where it is set

Main characters

What it is about

What I liked about the story

Who would like this book

Reviewer's name

Copymaster 54

Adverts

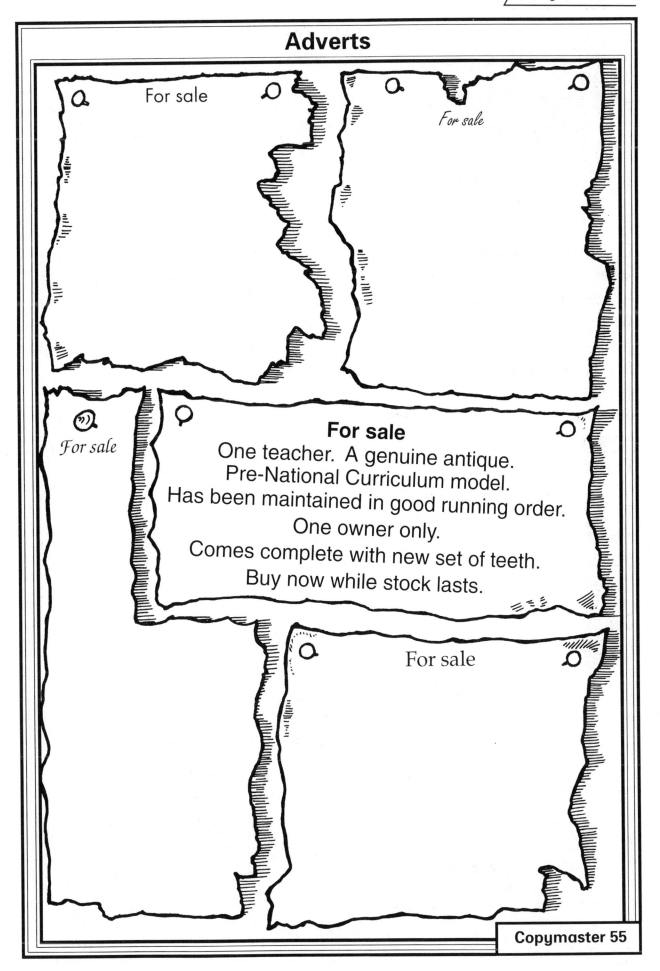

For sale

For sale

For sale

For sale
One teacher. A genuine antique.
Pre-National Curriculum model.
Has been maintained in good running order.
One owner only.
Comes complete with new set of teeth.
Buy now while stock lasts.

For sale

Layout

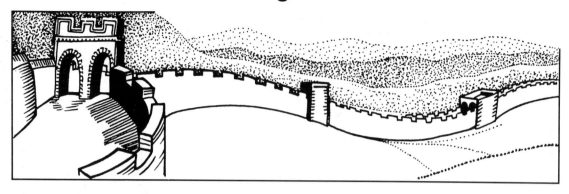

China is a large country. It reaches for more than 3000 kilometres. There are mountains, forests, deserts and tropical areas. The Great Wall of China was built to keep out invaders. At one time 30 000 men were working on the Wall. It is between 5 and 10 metres high. You can walk along the top of the wall. There are watch-towers along the wall. It was originally 6000 kilometres long. The Chinese believed that the Wall was really a dragon that had fallen asleep. The Chinese invented a number of different things that we still use today. They made gunpowder and used this to create the first fireworks. They also invented a strange-looking wheelbarrow. This was called the wooden ox. They floated magnets on bowls of water to act as compasses. They built giant water-clocks that rang out every quarter of an hour. Rich people in China ate a wide variety of foods. The poor people ate mainly vegetables, millet, rice, noodles and bread. They ate with chopsticks. The rich drank rice wine while the poor drank green tea.

Copymaster 56

66

Rewrite

Hurricanes and storms

On average there are approximately 45 000 storms reported to the meteorological offices of the world community every day. These storms play an important role in maintaining the balance of nature. They release excess energy, thereby restoring the balance of the atmosphere. The word 'hurricane' finds its origin in the Caribbean word meaning 'big wind'. Hurricanes can only occur where the sea is warm enough. The sea has to be about 27 degrees Celsius. Because of this phenomenon the colder regions of the world only occasionally have hurricanes. On average at least a dozen hurricanes begin each year in the Atlantic Ocean. Hurricanes have been known to spread over an area of 644 kilometres wide. In the centre of a hurricane is the calm 'eye'. The wind whirling round the eye of the storm can reach speeds of up to 320 kilometres per hour. In Galveston, Texas, a hurricane in 1900 caused tides so high that homes were flooded and 6000 people died. In 1970 in Bangladesh over half a million people were killed.

Copymaster 57

Information list

Ancient Egypt

In 5 000 BC farmers grew crops on the banks of the Nile.

They believed in life after death.

From 2 700 BC they built pyramids.

The pyramid at Saqqara was 62 metres high.

They mummified bodies to preserve them.

Villages and towns were ruled by kings called pharaohs.

In 2 450 BC the Great Pyramid of King Khufu was built.

They were buried with their possessions.

It took over 2 million bricks to build the Great Pyramid.

Pyramids were tombs for the pharaohs.

The Great Pyramid was 147 metres high.

Copymaster 58

Computer error 1

Wildlife Safari Park,
Kimpton,
Sussex.

the public.

and thank you for your kind words.

It is our aim to use the park

can survive.

I am pleased that you arrived

Yours sincerely,

You are right to point out that

to ensure that endangered species

If it is fun as well

I am writing to thank you

I am pleased that you enjoyed your visit

to the Wildlife Safari Park.

Dear Joanna,

we do run a conservation programme.

We aim to rehabilitate animals.

for your recent letter.

Jane Carter.

We also hope to educate

home safely from your visit

Once again

then that is an extra bonus.

Copymaster 59

Headings

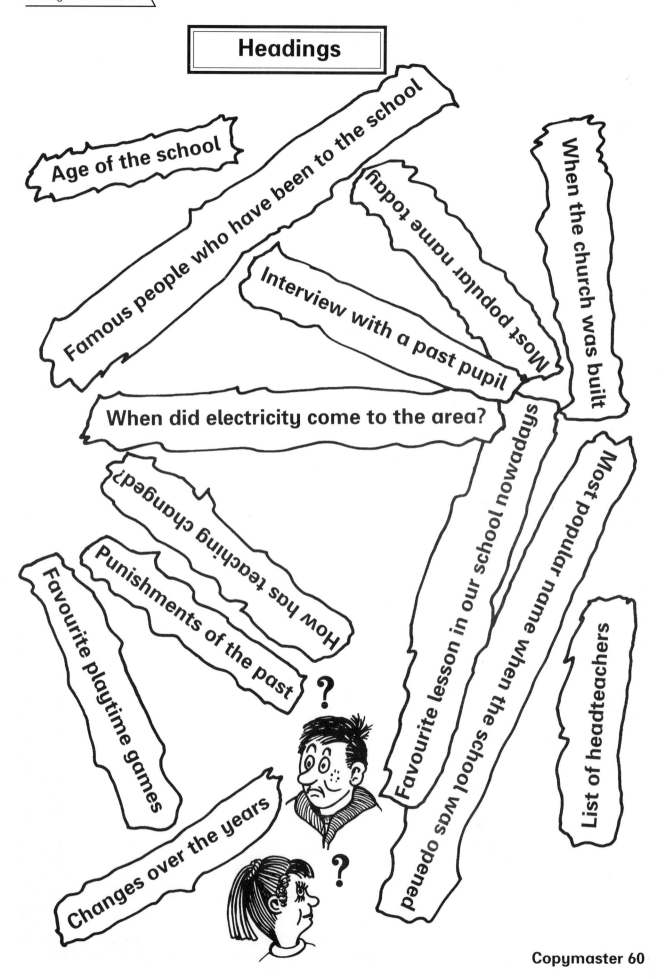

Age of the school

Famous people who have been to the school

Most popular name today

When the church was built

Interview with a past pupil

When did electricity come to the area?

How has teaching changed?

Punishments of the past

Favourite playtime games

Changes over the years

Favourite lesson in our school nowadays

Most popular name when the school was opened

List of headteachers

Copymaster 60

50-word items

STORM HITS SCHOOL

DOG FINDS TREASURE

Glossary and contents

Glossary

Contents

Glossary	Contents
Calpolli	The Aztec people
Chinampas	Aztec worship
Codices	Crafts
Maguey plant	Farming
Pulque	Clothing
	The Spanish
Tlazcalli	Food

Copymaster 62

72

WRITING FROM READING

This section focuses upon one important aspect of writing: that all writers develop through the influence of what they have read. Children are shown the importance of learning how to write from their reading – to find out how writers gain their effects by reading as a writer. Some of the copymasters require children to **imitate or emulate** a certain style or approach, while others require the children to **respond** to a piece of writing, sometimes jotting down ideas, thoughts and feelings, and at other times writing in various forms – letters, diary entries or stories.

Copymaster 63 (The playground)
Children should tell the story of what is happening in the picture. By talking or writing they could respond to specific questions: How does the teacher on duty feel? What has she seen happening? What is she thinking about? Pick on different incidents in the picture for the children to consider – they could give names to some of the children and then consider what they may be doing, who their friends are, why they are behaving in this way, what they are feeling and thinking, what they may be saying and what will happen next.

Copymaster 64 ('The White Bear')
There are a range of activities that could arise from this story. Children could circle all the wintry words and make a collection that could be added to. They could discuss why the man wanted to take the bear to the King and what the King might do when they arrived. The children could cut the story into sections, sticking them on to separate sheets of paper and then illustrating to make a simple book. The children could then continue by completing the story.

Copymaster 65 ('C Poem')
This poem should be carefully read aloud by the teacher. Children could then draw each item in the poem on the copymaster. They may then wish to choose other letters – I and O are easy ones to start with – and make a list of things that these letters are similar to. This could then be made into a list poem. For instance:

> O is a mouth singing,
> a party balloon in the sky,
> the sun in the summer,
> a two-penny piece,
> one of Dad's juggling balls,
> the steering wheel on our car,
> a beefburger,
> the middle of an egg …

Copymaster 66 ('In the Cold')
Again this poem could be illustrated, this time with drawings of the different animals. The children could write down how the poem makes them feel and what it makes them think of. This could then lead into children writing their own poems in imitation of the simple forms 'In the sun', 'In the rain', 'In the snow', 'In the wind', 'By the sea' and so on. For instance:

> In the sun –
> cows sleep by hedges.

> In the sun –
> sunbathers lie on their towels.

Copymaster 67 ('The Wise Man and the Tyrant')
This story is a good one to tell. The children should reread the copymaster and then begin by drawing the sequence of events as a cartoon. This will help them to visualise the story. The children should then try retelling the tale in pairs, helping each other. They should then practise in a larger circle, taking it in turns. This could be followed by children telling the story in pairs to children from another class. Other possible response activities include:

- Writing the diary of the faithful servant, describing the day when his master almost lost his head
- Writing a letter from someone in the crowd to a relative about what they saw
- Writing the story of what happened to the faithful servant next, continuing the tale from the copymaster
- Writing a list poem in which children imagine they have become the wealthiest person alive, listing what they would spend their money on. Joanne wrote:

> If I were so wealthy I would –
> feed the people of Somalia
> till their tummies were like drums,
> save the whale by buying the ocean
> and declaring it a whale-safe zone,
> build houses for the people
> who live in cardboard boxes,
> buy up all the zoos in the world
> and rebuild them so that the animals
> had plenty of space to roam in …

Copymaster 68 ('The Growler')
This is a true story. Children could jot down their initial responses – any thoughts, feelings or things they are reminded of. These could then be shared and discussed. Key questions to discuss may be: Why did the teacher do this? How did the little boy feel? What would the other children have thought? Writing in response could take

as its subject the boy telling his mum what had happened, the teacher telling another teacher, or the children pretending they were in the class and writing an account of the scene from their own viewpoint.

Copymaster 69 ('City Jungle')
Read the poem aloud carefully. The children should jot down their initial impressions and thoughts – how they felt, what it reminded them of. They should underline parts they did and did not like and bits that puzzled them. These should be compared and discussed. The children should underline or circle words that make the different objects sound like creatures. They should draw a picture showing some of the parts of the scene described. Their circled pictures and words should be compared. The children should then choose a place to write about – seaside, forest, river, village, estate, arcade, cinema, market, supermarket, station, etc. – and list the key objects they wish to put into the poem. They should then work at each object, using imagery to make them sound like something else – animals, birds, insects, fish, flowers, fruit, trees, plants, feelings, vegetables, etc. For instance:

> The sea crawls
> on its hands and knees
> spitting out stones.
>
> Rocks squat
> like toads waiting.
>
> Seaweed waves its hair.
> The wind clenches
> its icy teeth.

> The beach-huts stare
> as solemn as monks
> at the streak of horizon.
>
> Towels blossom,
> beachballs bloom.
>
> The waves chatter
> to themselves.

Copymaster 70 ('Wind Poem')
This poem was written after one of the great storms of the 1980s. The children should read the poem carefully and then jot down and discuss what picture the poem makes them imagine. The children should circle all the words that are powerful and that make the wind sound strong, and then underline all the rhymes and half-rhymes. Children should then compare what they have decided to underline/circle. This will give rise to fruitful discussion as to why certain words have been chosen or not. The children should then choose an aspect of the weather to write about, imitating the style of the poem yet choosing a set of words that are appropriate to the subject. So for a sun poem, hot words will be needed. For instance:

> Sun blisters the earth.
>
> The turf curls up,
> dry as toast.
>
> Sun withers flowers,
> showers evaporate.

FURTHER IDEAS ▶

Jotting down the first impressions and reactions to stories, poems, TV and radio programmes.

Writing notes about what you did and did not like, what puzzled you (what you do not quite understand, what questions you have or what you are curious about) and what patterns/connections you noticed? These four areas – likes, dislikes, puzzles and patterns – are fruitful topics for discussion and comparison. It is useful to encourage children to discuss the parts of stories and poems that puzzle them and talk their way towards deepening their understanding.

Writing a letter to a character in a story giving advice.

Making a family tree to show the characters in a story.

Drawing the picture that stays in children's heads after they've read a poem.

Drawing a map of the story.

Designing a front cover.

Reading a poem and guessing the (previously unseen) title.

Stopping at a key moment in a story and writing the thoughts that might be running through the main character's head. This key moment could be from the 'class novel' that the teacher is reading and could be a group or individual reading task. An example of a suitable key moment is in *The Hobbit*, when Bilbo is lost in the darkness and can hear Gollum. What thoughts might be running through his mind?

Drawing a time line to show the sequence of events in a story.

Writing a news report of events from a story or poem.

Jotting down feelings about a poem, character, place or event. Children should think about what the writing made them feel and what memories it stirred.

Keeping a diary for the main character in a book such as *The Hobbit*.

Writing an estate agent's brochure to sell a place from a story.

Writing an end-of-term report for the main character at the end of the story.

Making brief notes and discussing what changed in the story.

Interviewing a character from the story.

Cutting up a poem and letting the children reassemble it.

Commenting on a character or incident – 'How I see Gandalf' or 'What I think about …'

The playground

Copymaster 63

'The White Bear'

Once upon a time there was a man who had a white bear. Now this bear was so beautiful that the man decided he would take it to see the King.

When they set off it was summer and the sun warmed them on their way.

Soon it became autumn and the leaves fell from the trees.

Then it was winter and the snow fell thick and fast.

On Christmas Eve they came to a cottage in the woods. They were very cold and very hungry. They had not eaten for three days.

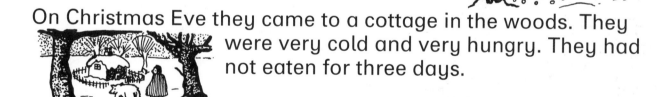

The snow crunched beneath their feet. It covered the trees. Its icy breath blew into their faces. They looked like white ghosts drifting through the forest.

So they knocked at the door of the cottage hoping for shelter.

Copymaster 64

'C Poem'

A cup, a chin,
the silver moon,
a bridge, a nose,
tip of a spoon.

A grin, a snail,
a shrimping net,
a giant's ear,
a snakey pet.

A monkey's smile
a finger nail,
a pirate's sword,
a fisherman's sail.

Copymaster 65

'In the Cold'

In the cold –
the badger hides in her set.

In the cold –
the robin fluffs out her feathers.

In the cold –
the dormouse curls into a ball.

In the cold –
the fox lies snug in his den.

In the cold –
the squirrel sleeps in her drey.

In the cold –
our cat creeps up to the fire.

In the cold –
we dress up warm and wish for the sun.

Copymaster 66

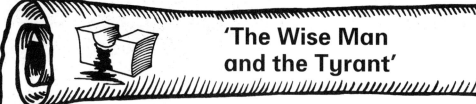

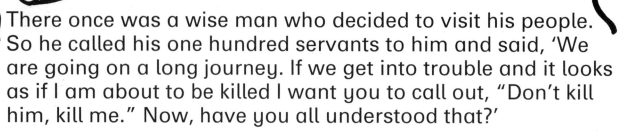

'The Wise Man and the Tyrant'

There once was a wise man who decided to visit his people. So he called his one hundred servants to him and said, 'We are going on a long journey. If we get into trouble and it looks as if I am about to be killed I want you to call out, "Don't kill him, kill me." Now, have you all understood that?'

His one faithful servant that was left behind said, 'Yes, oh Master.' So it was that the two of them visited many towns and villages till in the end they came to the main square of a city where the cruellest tyrant in the world lived. And the cruel tyrant was in a terrible temper.

'What are you looking at?' shouted the tyrant at the wise man. 'Oh, nothing' replied the wise man.
'I'm not "nothing". I'm a great King,' roared the tyrant. 'Off with his head.'

Soon a crowd had gathered to see the wise man have his head cut off. Just as the axe man was about to do his duty the faithful servant remembered what he had to say and shouted out, 'Don't kill him, kill me.' The tyrant was amazed and had the servant dragged to him. 'Why do you wish to be killed instead of this man?' asked the tyrant.

'I'm sorry,' said the wise man, 'but he has heard of the prophecy that states that on this very day, in this very place, the man who has his head chopped off will live for ever and become the richest and most powerful man in the world.

'Richest and most powerful!' shouted the tyrant. 'Live for ever!'

So it was that the cruellest tyrant in the world lay down his own head on the chopping block …

Copymaster 67

'The Growler'

When I was about five years old I had a teacher called Miss Woolett. She was tall and had very long golden hair. She had it piled up on her head and some of it hung down in ringlets. She was very pretty.

One afternoon we were standing round the piano singing when she stopped playing and looked at us.

'Now then, one of you is making a horrible growling noise,' she said. 'Which one of you is spoiling our song?'

I looked round to see who the culprit might be. When I looked back she was staring at me.

'Now, don't you sing anymore. Just open and close your mouth but I don't want to hear any sound come out at all.'

That afternoon I felt like a goldfish.

Copymaster 68

81

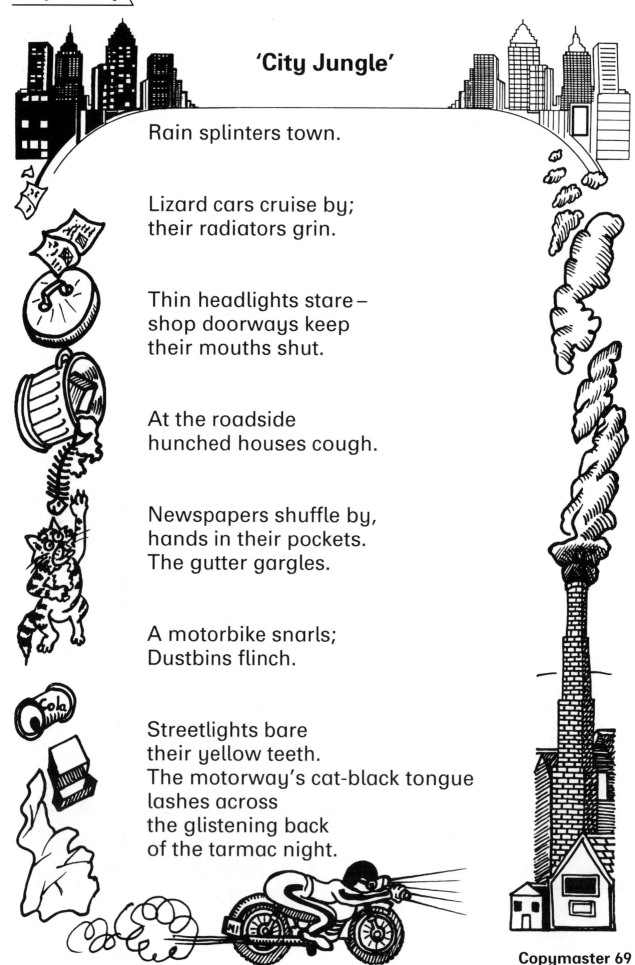

'City Jungle'

Rain splinters town.

Lizard cars cruise by;
their radiators grin.

Thin headlights stare –
shop doorways keep
their mouths shut.

At the roadside
hunched houses cough.

Newspapers shuffle by,
hands in their pockets.
The gutter gargles.

A motorbike snarls;
Dustbins flinch.

Streetlights bare
their yellow teeth.
The motorway's cat-black tongue
lashes across
the glistening back
of the tarmac night.

Copymaster 69

'Wind Poem'

Wind slices its icy blade.

Wind raids trees,
smacks leaves up back streets.

Wind somersaults sheets,
bustles and kicks.

Wind flexes muscles,
flicks its quivering wrist.

Wind twists dustbins
into clattering cartwheels.

Wind curls its steel tongue
like a shout flung at the sky.

Wind sighs;
Dies.

Copymaster 70

WRITING FROM PERSONAL EXPERIENCE

This brief section is concerned with ensuring that children's personal writing, formed directly from their own home experience, is not forgotten. Whilst many infant children are familiar with talking about their weekend 'news' on a Monday morning, this use of personal experience often dies out in the junior years. The copymasters in this section focus on the use of memory and explore the diary format.

Copymaster 71 (Memory time line 0–7 years)
Into each box the children draw a key memory. The copymaster can then be cut up and the drawings used as headings to pieces of writing that describe the memories. If they aren't yet old enough, the children could draw something they are looking forward to in the box. While children have no memory of years 0–2/3, they may well have gained second-hand knowledge about incidents that happened at this time, for example moving house or a baby brother being born. Children could fill in the copymaster with someone at home.

Copymaster 72 (Memory boxes)
This time the boxes have headings. The children draw a relevant memory into each box. What happened can be told to the teacher or a group, or the boxes can be cut up and used as illustrations to a written account.

Copymaster 73 (My diary)
Here the children use the questions to help them write an account of what happened yesterday.

Copymaster 74 (Memory time line 7–11 years)
This time line provides for key events for junior-age children. The children draw into each box a key memory from that age. The copymaster can be cut up and a 'Memory Poster' made, using the boxes as illustrations to written accounts about each memory. As before, children who aren't old enough can draw what they are looking forward to in coming years.

Copymaster 75 (Memory jogger)
Under each heading the children jot down any words or ideas that come with the relevant memory. It may help them if they close their eyes and try to 'see' the memory. Get the children to share their lists with a partner and to tell the story of some of their memories. This can then lead on to children circling the memory with the most potential for writing and submitting a written piece for inclusion in a book of class memories.

Copymaster 76 (Gnome's diary)
This copymaster shows a few pages from a gnome's diary. Using very small writing the children should try to complete the blank diary pages on the copymaster. They may wish to cut out the four diary spreads, sew them in the middle with one stitch (see Copymaster 84) and make a miniature book.

FURTHER IDEAS

'The funniest thing that has ever happened to me.'

'The saddest time I had.'

'A family row.'

'When I went to hospital/was ill.'

'My biggest fear is …'

'The best holiday we had …'

'The most important event in my life.'

'When Mum/Dad/Gran/Teacher got angry.'

'A time I cried.'

'What I do after school.'

'A new person in the family.'

'A pet we had.'

'Moving home.'

'First day at school.'

'Memories of the infants' school.'

'What I am looking forward to ...'

'What I am not looking forward to ...'

'A part of my work I find hard ...'

'Parts of my work that I enjoy ...'

'Personal Writing' books – these are private journals. The pieces of writing can be marked with a capital P which means they are private and will be read only by the teacher (not aloud to the class). The children are allowed to write on any subject they wish.

Memory time line
0–7 years

1 year old	2 years old	3 years old	4 years old

5 years old	6 years old	7 years old

Copymaster 71

86

Memory boxes

Best holiday

A funny time

A sad time

When I was angry

In trouble

Copymaster 72

  **My diary**

| 1 2 3 4 5 6 7 |
| 8 9 10 11 12 13 14 |
| 15 16 17 18 19 20 21 |
| 22 23 24 25 26 27 28 |
| 29 30 31 |

What was yesterday's date?

When did you get up that morning?

What did you have for breakfast?

What did you do in the morning?

What did you do at lunchtime?

What did you do in the afternoon?

Who did you play with?

What was the weather like?

What was the best thing that happened?

What was the worst thing that happened?

What were you looking forward to?

Copymaster 73

Memory time line 7–11 years

7 years old	8 years old	9 years old

10 years old	11 years old

Copymaster 74

89

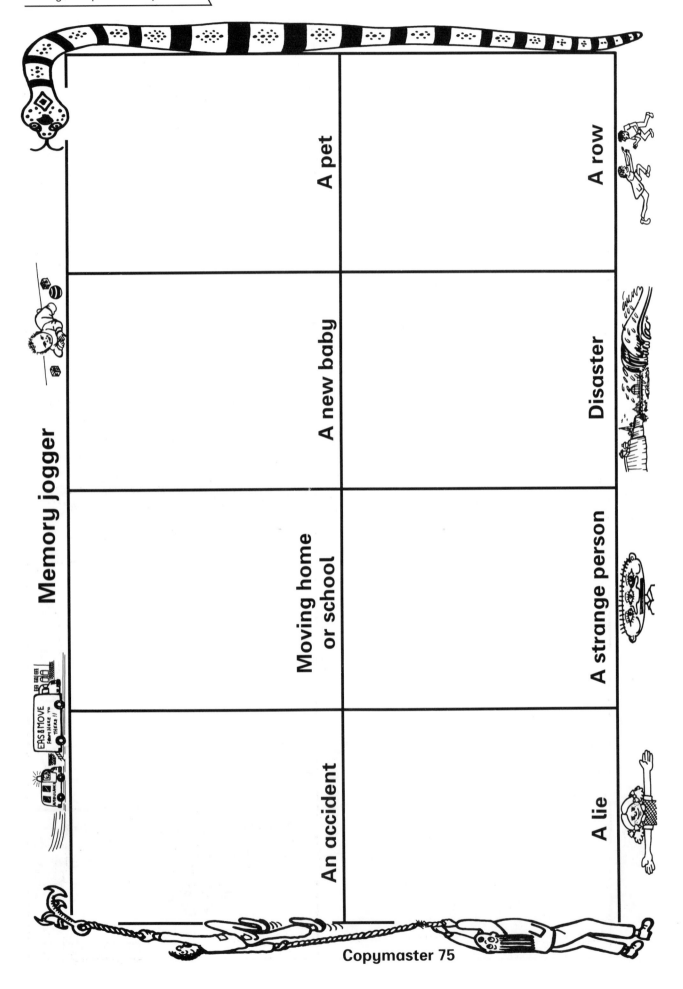

Memory jogger

A pet	A new baby	Moving home or school	An accident

A row	Disaster	A strange person	A lie

Copymaster 75

90

Gnome's diary

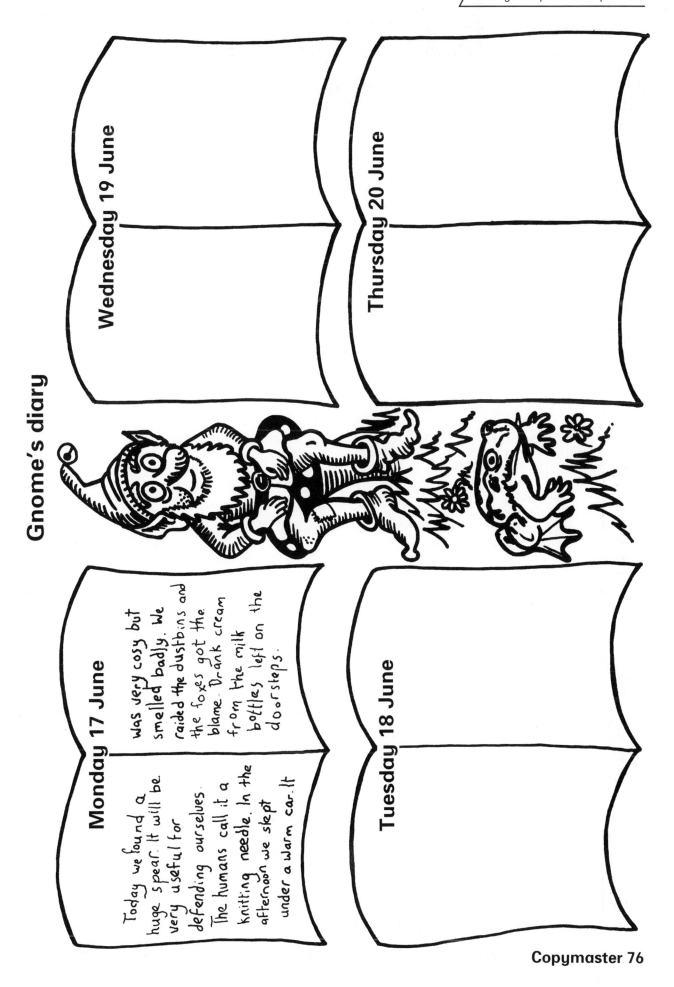

Wednesday 19 June

Thursday 20 June

Monday 17 June

Today we found a huge spear. It will be very useful for defending ourselves. The humans call it a knitting needle. In the afternoon we slept under a warm car. It was very cosy but smelled badly. We raided the dustbins and the foxes got the blame. Drank cream from the milk bottles left on the doorsteps.

Tuesday 18 June

REDRAFTING AND PROOFREADING

This final section is concerned with developing the process of writing and looks at the importance of redrafting as a way of improving what has been written. Copymasters focus upon making texts more interesting through the careful selection of words and structure. The children are invited to improve first drafts of stories and poetry, and to write from a brainstorming session. The skills of proofreading are also highlighted through exercises that require punctuation and spelling to be checked.

Copymaster 83 directs children into the early stages of using a response partner to assist in redrafting and proofreading. There is also help with making a simple book and a chance for children to invite their families to help them with writing. There are two self-assessment copymasters for children to choose from; for the teacher **Copymaster 97** (Writing record) could be used for every child and maintained as part of official school records. It is suggested that this is used each term to assist in recording what the child can do and to focus the teacher's mind on what is needed next to assist development. **Copymaster 98** (Writing record prompt sheet) has key words on it that may be useful when completing the writing record. The words on the prompt sheet should be updated in terms of National Curriculum requirements as and when changes are made to Level Descriptions/Statements of Attainment and National Assessments.

Copymaster 77 (Boring sentences 1)
The children read the sentences and then make changes to improve them and make them more interesting. The children could do any of the following:

● **Change** a word – so 'The tramp came down the road' becomes 'The tramp hobbled down the road'
● **Add in** words – so 'The tramp hobbled down the road' becomes 'The old tramp hobbled down the dusty road'
● **Add on** words – so 'The tramp came down the road' becomes 'The tramp came down the road shouting for joy'.

The children should compare their sentences to see who has made the best improvements. The first one has been done for them.

Copymaster 78 (Capitals, full stops and 'and')
This is the start of Simon's story. He has used too many 'and's. Let the children change his writing to get rid of some of these 'and's and add in full stops and capital letters. This could be done individually, after which children could compare and discuss so that agreement can be reached on what should be changed.

Copymaster 79 (Fill the gaps)
To practise selecting words carefully the children, in pairs, read the passage and then insert what they feel may be the most effective word. Pairs should compare and discuss their choices. Some of the spaces might be filled by one word, some by two or three.

Copymaster 80 (Poem draft 1)
This copymaster shows the first draft of a poem. The children have to read it through and then make any changes they wish to, in order to help improve it. Changes should then be discussed and justified. The children should focus on changing words to improve them.

Copymaster 81 (Story draft 1)
This copymaster is a first draft of the opening to a story. On this draft children should make changes to improve the story. In particular they should look out for repetition and add in words for description.

Copymaster 82 (Speech bubbles)
Children should look carefully at the pictures on this copymaster and then add in what they think the people are saying. This activity should be built on at Key Stage 2 by children circling the actual words that their characters speak when they write. Individuals or groups should be shown how to set out speech marks once they can identify which words a character says.

Copymaster 83 (Response partner)
A response partner is used to test out a piece of writing. The idea is that once the children have written a first draft they read their work to a friend who will be their response partner. The response partner has to let the child know what works well in their piece of writing as well as helping them make any improvements. The directions on the copymaster should prove useful in establishing response partners in the classroom. Once the children have used their response partners to help with the revising they can then work together on the proofreading. Point out to the children that they should check their writing with the teacher before publishing!

This activity helps children to develop the ability to revise their own work and to critically comment on the strengths and weaknesses of writing. The children may wish to fill in suggestions at the bottom of the page following a discussion on what helps most when working together. The filled-in copymaster should then be kept as a reminder of the procedure.

Copymaster 84 (Make a book)
This copymaster gives simple instructions for making a booklet and could be used in school or taken home for parents to help in the activity.

Copymaster 85 (Family story)
This copymaster is an invitation for people at home, whether families or friends, to write a story with the children. The children could begin the story, with those at home then joining in and adding more writing as well as illustrations. These stories could be discussed in school and would make an interesting book or scrapbook collection – especially for parents to see on parents' evenings.

Copymaster 86 (My writing)
This is a self-assessment sheet for younger children to complete by colouring in the appropriate face and adding their name, the date and their comments on their own favourite piece of writing.

Copymaster 87 (Brainstorm)
This copymaster shows a handwritten brainstorming session for stimulating a piece of writing on owls. The children need to think carefully about the intended audience (this could be written for another class or to take home) and the main pieces of information that are mentioned before they use the brainstorm as a basis for their own writing. Children should decide whether they need to include all the information shown on the brainstorm and whether to include illustrations as well as writing.

The second half of the copymaster contains a blank brainstorming model for the children to use when gathering information on a writing topic of the teacher's or their own choice.

Copymaster 88 (Boring sentences 2)
The children should read and then improve these sentences by making **changes** to dull words, **adding in** words to improve description and **adding on** words to extend the description. They should beware of adding too much, which could detract from the quality of the writing.

Copymaster 89 (Boring words)
This is a copy of Joanna's opening to a story. The children should focus upon improving the **choice** of words by redrafting, making changes on the copymaster first.

Copymaster 90 (Proofread)
The children should proofread this story opening, checking carefully for spelling mistakes and adding capital letters, full stops, speech marks and paragraphs. They could then complete the story.

Copymaster 91 (Computer error 2)
This copymaster should be used like a cloze procedure. My computer has lost some of the words and phrases from this story. The children should discuss and decide what are the best words to use to fill in the gaps – sometimes two or three words are needed. Children could then complete the story.

Copymasters 92 and 93 (Poem drafts 2 and 3)
These copymasters show the first drafts of two new poems. The children should work over the drafts in pairs, improving the quality by writing in the spaces between the lines, crossing out words and underlining or circling parts they wish to improve.

Copymasters 94 and 95 (Story drafts 2 and 3)
These copymasters show the first drafts of parts of a story. The children should work over the drafts, polishing the prose by making changes on the copymasters. These changes should then be discussed as a class. **Copymaster 95** also needs proofreading for spelling mistakes and punctuation.

Copymaster 96 (Self-assessment)
This copymaster could be used at the end of each term for older children to summarise how they consider they have developed as writers and how they would like to develop in the future. The copymaster could be used as part of the termly 'writing conference' (see pages ix–x). The teacher will need to discuss with the children during a class session the sorts of things they might write on their sheets. It may be useful to attach the copymaster to an example of the child's work.

Copymaster 97 (Writing record)
This copymaster may be used by the teacher to make notes on the child's on-going development, informed by termly discussions with the child (see the notes on the writing conference on pages ix–x) and general classroom observations. **Copymaster 98** acts as a prompt sheet to help the teacher complete this record.

The writing record can be used for children who have just begun to write as well as experienced writers. The teacher will need to listen carefully to children talking to gain a sense of their ability to compose and to fill in the 'content' section. In the 'conventions' section the teacher may wish to distinguish between the various spelling stages – scribbling, letter shapes, using properly formed letters, sound/symbol correspondence, spelling using phonics, spelling from visual memory. The teacher may wish to note whether children play at and enjoy writing. Do children know the difference between drawing and writing? Can they read back their own writing?

Copymaster 98 (Writing record prompt sheet)
This copymaster highlights key considerations and aspects to look for when completing the termly writing record on **Copymaster 97**. Teachers may wish to add in key words or phrases from the Level Descriptions/ Statements of Attainment to assist in the on-going monitoring of children's development in terms of the National Curriculum. They may also wish to add any key aspects that National Assessments are highlighting.

FURTHER IDEAS

Write in front of the children on an easel, flipchart, board or OHP. As you reread what has been written encourage the children to suggest improvements.

Draw children's attention to well-used words and phrases they come across in their reading.

Create worksheets of poorly written pieces of writing that need improving.

Encourage children to reread and make improvements to their own writing.

Read out aloud examples of children's work and ask for suggestions to improve weaker parts.

Encourage the children to work in story circles. In the circle the children take it in turn to read aloud their stories while their friends make suggestions for improvement.

Create worksheets that focus on different proofreading aspects – speech marks, paragraphs, capital letters, etc. Use these to highlight features that certain children need to address in their own writing. Encourage children to check their writing for a limited number of such features.

Boring sentences 1

1   The dog came down the street.

The brown dog ran yapping down the high street.

2   The girl picked up the ball.

3   He said that he had seen a horse.

4   The apples were nice.

5   The snow fell on the trees.

6   The cat sat on me.

7   The bus went through the tunnel.

8   In the cave it was dark.

Copymaster 77

Full stops and 'and'

The cruel crow

early one morning sam went out and saw a crow and the crow was sitting in a tree and waiting and Simon went back to the house for his breakfast and the crow saw him go into the house and thought now I can fly down and pinch some beans from the garden and he flew down and pecked the beans and peapods and just at that moment simon came out of the house and he saw the crow and he tried to shoo it away and the crow did not like this and it pecked simon on the nose and simon got really angry

Copymaster 78

96

Fill the gaps

Sally had _____ wanted a puppy. When it was
her _____ birthday her Dad took her to the
_____ shop. He bought her a _____
puppy.

Sally called the _____ Noodles. It had a
_____ nose and a _____ tail.

That afternoon she took Noodles for a _____ in
the park. She had _____ ball to throw for
Noodles. But he wouldn't _____ back. He had run
away. Sally searched _____ for Noodles.

When she got home Sally had been _____. But as
she came up the path to her house who should come
_____ out to meet her? Yes, it was naughty
Noodles.

Copymaster 79

Poem draft 1

The big snow flakes fall

on the ground

they look like big lumps

as they drop down.

Snow covers the cars

in a cover of snow.

It is like white powder

on the lawn.

The puddles are frozen

and look like icy plates.

The snow crunches

beneath my feet.

The cat leaves small paw prints

and she comes home.

Copymaster 80

 **Story draft 1**

Once upon a time there was a woman who was lonely. She lived all by herself in the middle of a wood. She was quite lonely. She had no one to talk to from morning till night. She lived all by herself in a cottage in the middle of a wood.

Late one night she was in her sitting room. She had just lit a candle. The flame was moving and the shadows were moving. She moved across the room and she picked up her embroidery. She was making a pretty lace handkerchief. It was pretty.

She sat in front of the fire and watched the shadows move. The flames were moving. She picked up her pretty embroidery and began to sew. As she sewed she heard a big noise. It came from the roof. It sounded like someone with big feet was moving on the big roof. She wondered what on earth was going on.

Copymaster 81

Speech bubbles

Response partner

How to be a good response partner

1 Together, read your friend's writing carefully.

2 Now point out all the words, ideas and parts that you think are good.

3 Ask questions about the writing.

4 Point out any places where you think the writing could be made better.

5 Discuss ideas for changes and let the writer make the final decision.

Once the work has been redrafted, it needs to be proofread.

1 Put a circle around any spelling mistakes. Check these in a word book, dictionary or ask a friend.

2 Underline any places where you think the punctuation (full stops, capitals, question marks, speech marks) is wrong. Correct it.

3 Discuss the layout to make the work easy to read and attractive to look at.

Now your writing is ready to **publish**.

Copymaster 83

Make a book

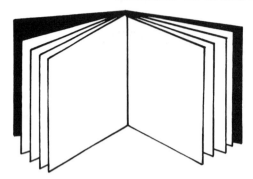

1 Take some sheets of paper and put a cover on the outside. Fold them carefully.

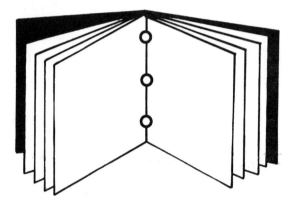

2 Make three holes.

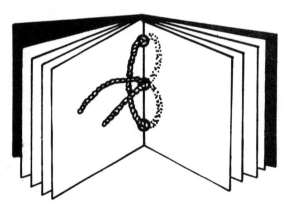

3 Sew the pages together.

4 Tie a knot in the thread.

Copymaster 84

Family story

Dear

We are writing to ask you to join in with our 'Family Story'. We are starting a story in school and we would like to ask you and members of your family – or friends – to add to the story and finish it. You may want to add illustrations. We have begun the story at the bottom of this page. When all the stories are finished we will display them in school. Thank you for becoming writers with us.

From,

_____

_____

_____

_____

_____

_____

_____

_____

_____

_____

_____

_____

Copymaster 85

My writing

Name –
Date –

I enjoy writing – stories

news

information

letters

poems

about myself

about school

I can – write neatly

join up

spell most words

use a dictionary

use a word book

use full stops

use capital letters

use question marks

I can – redraft

proofread

My best piece of writing is about –

I like it because –

Brainstorm

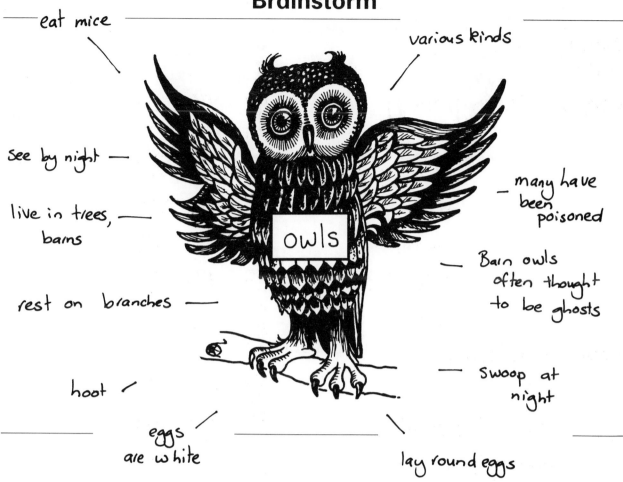

eat mice

various kinds

see by night

live in trees, barns

many have been poisoned

Barn owls often thought to be ghosts

rest on branches

hoot

swoop at night

eggs are white

lay round eggs

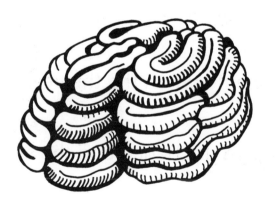

Boring sentences 2

1   The farmer looked at the bull as it came towards him.

2   The spacecraft door opened and out came a creature.

3   The waves banged on the rocks.

4   A car came round the corner.

5   George ran after the man.

6   The dog showed its teeth and growled.

7   The moon shone down on the thieves.

8   The boat came up the beach and the smugglers dropped out.

9   In my dream I saw a shape.

10   The teacher spoke to the noisy class.

Copymaster 88

Boring words

There was no noise in the classroom. On the wall was a drawing of a big monster with a big mouth full of big teeth. Suddenly it winked its horrid eye at me. It came alive and got off the wall. It came across the room and went through the window. Joel and I went after it.

We found it by the swings. It said in a funny voice, 'Leave me alone'. Now we were closer we could see it had funny bits of hair on it. Its eyes looked odd too. It was quite small with nice feet like a bird's. It smiled at us. Its teeth were not straight. 'I am fed up,' it said in a low voice. It started to cry.

Copymaster 89

Proofread

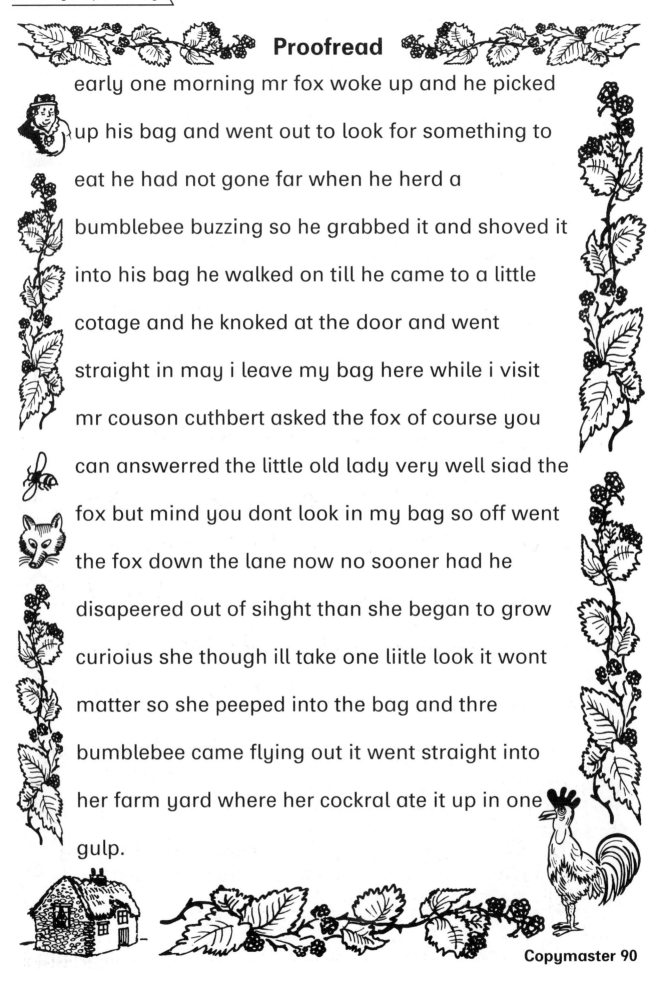

early one morning mr fox woke up and he picked up his bag and went out to look for something to eat he had not gone far when he herd a bumblebee buzzing so he grabbed it and shoved it into his bag he walked on till he came to a little cotage and he knoked at the door and went straight in may i leave my bag here while i visit mr couson cuthbert asked the fox of course you can answerred the little old lady very well siad the fox but mind you dont look in my bag so off went the fox down the lane now no sooner had he disapeered out of sihght than she began to grow curioius she though ill take one liitle look it wont matter so she peeped into the bag and thre bumblebee came flying out it went straight into her farm yard where her cockral ate it up in one gulp.

Copymaster 90

Computer error 2

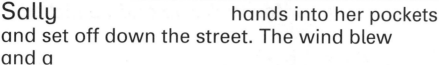

Sally   hands into her pockets and set off down the street. The wind blew and a

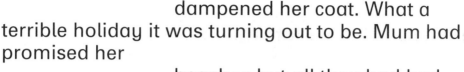

dampened her coat. What a terrible holiday it was turning out to be. Mum had promised her

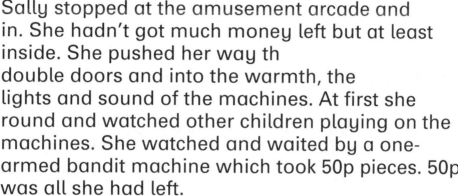

beaches but all they had had was rain and pebbly beaches covered in and crisp packets.

Sally stopped at the amusement arcade and in. She hadn't got much money left but at least inside. She pushed her way th double doors and into the warmth, the lights and sound of the machines. At first she round and watched other children playing on the machines. She watched and waited by a one-armed bandit machine which took 50p pieces. 50p was all she had left.

A boy with 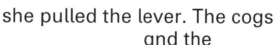 hair had been playing on the machine and when he left it Sally moved forwards to

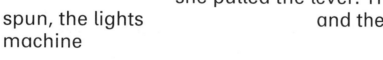 She pushed the coin into the slot and

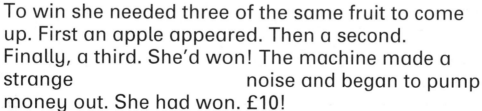 she pulled the lever. The cogs spun, the lights  and the machine

To win she needed three of the same fruit to come up. First an apple appeared. Then a second. Finally, a third. She'd won! The machine made a strange noise and began to pump money out. She had won. £10!

She left the arcade with her pockets and her with the excitement. She couldn't tell her mum. She disapproved of gambling. What on earth was she to do?

Copymaster 91

Poem draft 2

Park Walk in Winter

My teeth are cold.

The snow lies on the park.

It makes the pond white.

The ducks look for food

or stand still as still.

A cold wind blows

the trees all shake.

Snow drops off them.

Some small sparrows look

for bits of food.

A dog comes running by

chased by a small boy

her cheeks like fire.

Lorries and cars go by

their exhausts like

bright puffs of smoke.

But the park is dead quiet.

Copymaster 92

110

Poem draft 3

Follow me

Follow me to a place

where the trees have loads of fruit.

Follow me to a land

where there are lots of big trees

that all can move and talk to you.

Follow me to a country

where even the hedges are smiling at everybody.

Follow me to a world

that is made of all the funny things

that have been going on around here.

Follow me to a room

where the curtains hold each other's hands.

Follow me to a house

where the pots and pans are running

about everywhere saying things.

Copymaster 93

Story draft 2

The streets were empty but Sally thought that she was being followed. She thought that she could hear the noises of someone who was following her all the time. She turned around now and then but she could not see anyone. At the corner of South Street she went round quickly and hid behind a big dustbin. She could hear her heart beating as she was crouching down. She was trying to hold her breath. Then she heard the sound of someone's footsteps coming down the road quietly. Whoever it was paused by the big dustbin. Sally could see a pair of black shoes. They were smelly. She felt really scared in case she was spotted. Suddenly a hand shot down and grabbed her by the collar. She was pulled to her feet and a horrid face pressed close to hers. 'Now, tell me where it is,' asked the person. But Sally hadn't got the faintest clue what she was talking about.

Copymaster 94

Story draft 3

Tom ran down to the classroom but he was very late. Mrs Snell had already begun the lessin. He tried to creep in without being seen but she roared at him what on earth are you doing arriving so late Im soory he replide but the bus was late. She made a noise of disgust and so he sat down in his seat, sitting next to him was a girl that he had never seen before she had long black hair tied into a pigtale. Toms fingers wanted to pull it like a church bell pull. Mrs snell was telling them what to do and the girl next to tom was already writing loads. he looked over at what she was doing and saw that it was a story. it could of been really good but tom knudged her and ink spilt across the table and all across her work it also dropped onto her new school clothes. She turned to tom with her eyes burning with crossness You idiot she shouted. The next thing they new Mrs Snell had walked over to them

Copymaster 95

Self-assessment

| GOOD ← | OK | BAD |

List the types of writing that you prefer

Punctuation checklist
Paragraphs ☐
Speech marks ☐
Commas ☐
Exclamation marks ☐
Question marks ☐
Capital letters ☐
Full stops ☐
Apostrophes ☐

Name your best piece and say why you like it

Can you change your writing depending on who you are writing for? ☐

Do you plan before writing? ☐

How do you help as a response partner?

Can you redraft your own work? ☐

Can you proofread? ☐

Is your best writing neat? ☐

What sort of writing do you have the best ideas for?

Do you use the wordprocessor for writing? ☐

What is the next aspect you would like to improve?

How can your teacher help?

Any other comments about yourself as a writer?

Copymaster 96

Writing record

Name   Date

Title of writing

Context

Child's response

Content

Conventions

Process

Suggested level

Next development

Writing record prompt sheet

Context
Was this aided or unaided? Was this a first draft?

Child's response
Does the child enjoy writing/discussing writing?

Content
Good ideas, logical and chronological flow, appropriate style, good use of story grammar (well-described setting, engaging opening, believable characters, interesting events, a main dilemma, defined ending), engages interest, appropriate for purpose and audience? Is writing lively, honest, vigorous? Does the child play with language to create verbal effects? Does the child use imagery? Are the stories and poems moving? Is information writing clear and interesting? Is writing confident? Is writing structured effectively? Is the child's use of vocabulary appropriate, broad and interesting? Does the child write honestly and directly, convey meaning clearly and effectively, produce sustained and well-organised writing.

Conventions
Spelling stage, handwriting, punctuation (full stops, capitals, question marks, exclamation marks, commas, speech marks). Command of Standard English? Can the child set out a letter? Use of appropriate layout/paragraphs? Has the child moved beyond using 'and' repeatedly? Use of sentences in which subject/verb agree? Use of parts of speech correctly and effectively?

Process
Can the child redraft? Can the child spot areas that are effective and identify areas that could be improved, make improvements independently, discuss writing and justify redraftings, identify spelling, punctuation and grammar mistakes? Does the child proofread and make effective changes? Does the child plan and use a range of strategies for starting writing? Is the child a good response partner? Does the child use appropriate terms to discuss their writing?

Suggested level
Using the evidence of the child's writing during this term suggest the relevant NC level. Use the notes from any national assessment as guidance for the key determining factors.

Next development
Discuss and identify several areas for development with the child. Review these at the next conference session.

Copymaster 98